Acknowledgements

First and foremost, I give special thanks to my dear friend Terry Hill who painstakingly worked on the 'dissection' of the Seal of Truth; known as the Sigilum dei Aemeth. He managed to turn a 'flat earth' sigil into 7 exciting 2 dimensional images for our aspirants to be absorbed into.

To Caroline Wise a long-standing friend who works tirelessly for the Pagan network throughout Europe and North America, I thank her for her time and patience reading through this book and making constructive suggestions – all of which I took on board.

I wish also to thank Aaron Leitch for his invaluable input regarding the Angelical language, but most importantly of all, his creation of the Grand Seal of Earth attributed to Uri'el. The methods for making these Seals are not well known –according to other angelical masters they admit they do not know how many of them were made at all. However, what principles Aaron does know, he has followed in the making of this new Grand Seal. It may or may not stand up to the test of time, but it will certainly work for our purposes. But, I feel it could become THE Grand Seal of Earth.

Contents

Acknowledgements 3
   Contents 4
Preface 7
Introduction 11
Author's Note 21
   Practical Matters 22
   For less experienced 23
   Cleansing 24
   Angelic altar and tools 24
   The Angel 26
   Meditation 27
1 Archangel Luc'ifer 'Carrier of the Light' 29
   Legend 29
   First version 31
   Second version 32
   Path to Archangel Luc'ifer 34
2 Archangel Mikh'ael 'Who is as God' 43
   Legend 43
   Path to Archangel Mikh'ael 48
   The Conjuration 52
3 Archangel Gabri'el 'God is my strength' 61
   Legend 61
   Path To Gabri'el 65
   Conjuration 68
4 Archangel Sama'el 'Venom of God' 77
   Legend 77

Angelic Magick

A Guide To Angelic Beings
And How To Walk With Them

Judith Page

Preface by Aaron Leitch

978-1-906958-47-3

Copyright © Judith Page & Mandrake of Oxford 2012

All rights reserved. No reproduction, copy or transmission of this publication may be made without written permission. No paragraph of this publication may be reproduced, copied or transmitted without permission or in accordance with the provision of the copyright act of 1956 (as amended).

Dedicated to Alain Leroy, Lucifer, Pagan and Soutekh.

Other books by Judith Page

The Song of Set

Song of Meri-Khem

Song of Bast

Theft of the 7 Ankhs

Pathworking with the Egyptian Gods

Invoking the Egyptian Gods

Path To Sama'el 'Venom of God' 82
5 Archangel Rapha'el 'God has healed' 93
    Legend 93
    Path to Rapha'el 99
6 Archangel Zadki'el 'Righteousness of God' 109
    Legend 109
    Path to Zadki'el 114
7 Archangel Ana'el 'Joy of God' 125
    Legend 125
    Path to Ana'el 130
8 Archangel Cassi'el 'Speed of God' 141
    Legend 141
    Path to Cassi'el 146
9 Archangel Uri'el 'Flame of God' 157
    Legend 157
    Path to Uri'el 163
10 Enoch and the Watchers 171
    Legend 171
    Path to Enoch 178
Alphabets to use 197
    Theban 197
    Celestial 198
Chart of Angel Hours 201
Notes on The Seal of Truth 203
Bibliography 205

Preface

The book you are now holding is unique. To be certain, there is no shortage of books available on the subject of angels. They have been a source of curiosity and fascination for thousands of years - catching the interest of everyone from mystics and the faithful to scholars of religious and artistic history. They have been viewed as a source of fear and awe, of peace and hope, as the agents of creation and destruction and much, much more. For the authors of the Old Testament, the angels were divine messengers bearing God's blessings or wrath to the Earth. For the scholar-mystics of the Renaissance, they were the keepers of the hidden mysteries of nature and the muses of invention. More recently, the rise of the New Age movement saw the angels recast as kindly fairy-like beings of joy and happiness, charged most specifically with the guardianship of children and all things representing love and kindness.

This later New Age view of the angels - often derided as "fluffy bunny" - has dominated the subject of angelology for several decades. And it has been the basis for most of the thousands of angel books published in the last century. There have been tales of angels walking among us, appearing in times of desperate need, rescuing the unwary from danger, reuniting lovers, etc. All angels, so say these books, represent only goodness and kindness and wish for you to be happy in life.

Missing entirely are the wrathful beings that destroyed Sodom and Gomorrah (Genesis 19), wrestled with prophets (Genesis 32) and slew firstborn children (Exodus 12). We see no mention of cosmic entities with bestial faces (Ezekiel 1, Revelation 4), who will destroy the world (Revelation 7, etc), or even the *ha Sathan* who accuses men of wrongdoing and visits divine judgment upon the wicked (Book of Job).

It is not surprising that modern spiritual seekers would wish to focus entirely upon the angels of mercy and peace. Yet, this is a very one-sided view of angelic beings and what they mean to humanity. The angels are the governors of the cosmos and directors of the motions of stars and planets. They are the divine agents of creation, which also makes them the agents of destruction and renewal. They are infinitely wise and balanced beings who can act from a position of divine mercy or divine wrath as needed.

Today, the "fluffy" view of angels is giving way to a more balanced view. We now recognize that angels are not little fairies who grant our wishes, but are in fact vast and powerful - and even dangerous. We are turning to older sources for information about them: perhaps most importantly the medieval books of angel magick called "grimoires." Books such as *The Key of Solomon the King*, *The Heptameron*, *The Almadel of Solomon*, the *Pauline Arts* and dozens of other classical books of magick were written by mystics who fully understood the true power of the angelic hosts.

Most importantly, the grimoires preserve methods for establishing contact with such beings. One does not boldly enter the company of angels and start making demands! Instead, it is necessary to meet them, get to know them and *establish working relationships with them*. Only then should one be so foolhardy as to ask the angels for help or enlightenment. Otherwise, why should such beings know or care about your needs? Sadly, this aspect of working with angels has been sorely lacking from most modern books on the subject.

And that is what makes this book so unique. The information you will find here is not drawn from sensationalized tales of angel encounters, or from television shows about helpful fallen angels hoping to earn their wings. This book draws symbols and imagery from the same classical sources described above. It includes the seals and sigils and sacred imagery that has been associated with the angels for hundreds and (in some cases) thousands of years. It treats the angels properly, as cosmic entities in charge of all of creation who can unlock gateways to greater and deeper spiritual experiences for the aspirant. Best of all, it provides a method by which the aspirant can establish first contact with the angels in relative safety.

Those of you who already work with the Solomonic grimoires and their decidedly Old Testament-style angels might mistakenly overlook this book. Rather than complex summoning rituals (as we find in the medieval texts) this book focuses upon a series of guided visualizations. And because such visualizations are a hallmark of the New Age, you might mistake this for just another pop angel book with little practical usefulness. However, I urge you to take a closer look:

New Age angelology tends to focus on feel-good imagery - while the visualizations here draw their imagery from classical grimoires and Kabbalistic philosophy. Plus, they have a specific and *useful* goal. Each visualization takes you on a journey into the symbolic realm of an archangel, where you are introduced to the entity's sigils and symbols and other sacred imagery before encountering the archangel himself. Each visualization builds upon those before it, until the aspirant has been led through the seven circles of heaven and has established a personal link to the archangel that governs each one. At the end, the aspirant will have learned to recognize the images, seals and symbols they will encounter in the Solomonic and other advanced systems of angel summoning.

Such guided visualizations are certainly absent from the medieval texts about angels. So, why should I urge *anyone* who wishes to work with angels - even Solomonic practitioners - to follow the instructions in this book? Simply put, this book is based upon the same principle I described above: *safely establishing first contact*. These visualizations are focused upon meeting each archangel for the first time, and then building a working relationship with that archangel. Yet it accomplishes this without resort to the full-fledged summoning ceremonies intended to call the angel down to the physical plane - an advanced practice the grimoires tend to jump into without preamble.

I believe these guided visualizations are a wonderful way for the novice to begin their path with the angels. If you complete this course, you will find that you have gained a familiarity with the entities that you will later call upon for help. Both you and the angel in question will have already met, and the angel will know that you are a sincere spiritual seeker worthy of his attentions.

This book even includes simple rituals by which you can submit petitions to the archangels in times of need - and these rituals are not entirely removed from the methods of the grimoires. Therefore, working through the steps outlined in this book can serve as a wonderful bridge between "square one" and the fully adept practices of angelic summoning.

I wish you much success on your journey to become familiar with the angels of nature.

Zorge,

Aaron Leitch

January 2012

Aaron Leitch is one of today's foremost practitioners and authors on the subject of angel magick, both traditional and modern. You can find his books and essays at his homepage: http://kheph777.tripod.com/

You can also visit his blog *Ananael* (Secret Wisdom) - where he posts new material, instructional essays, upcoming events and much more: http://aaronleitch.wordpress.com/

Introduction

> 'An angel can illumine the thought and mind of man by strengthening the power of vision, and by bringing within his reach some truth which the angel himself contemplates.' St. Thomas Aquinas

Mysticism and spirituality is about trusting our experience, and today it is possible that we are being asked to trust our experience of angels.

Thomas Aquinas, the thirteenth century priest, professor and philosopher said: 'The universe would not be complete without angels. . . The entire corporal world is governed by God through the angels.'

For those who have felt an angelic presence in their lives, suggests that angels do not have to be believed in, as the experience is enough to tell us, that it is not a matter of belief, but a matter of experience.

Over the last few centuries, there has been no room for angels, and certainly no room for mystics. As we move away from machine cosmology, it is inevitable that the mystics together with angels are returning because a living cosmology is coming back.

When someone mentions the word 'angel' we automatically conjure up images of beautiful creatures depicted in religious art of the Renaissance period.

But how exactly did images of winged beings find their way into the hearts, minds and symbolic forms of man? Where did the notion of 'angel' come from before that?

We could begin with the Sumerians; this, after all is the oldest recorded civilization that has left us clear evidence of the use of the winged human motif. But winged figures go back much further than Sumer; in fact the image almost certainly goes back into the shamanic mists of time.

Sumerian culture flourished around 3,000 BCE between the Tigris and Euphrates Rivers in what is present-day Iraq, these people had a complex religion that embraced a wide variety of gods and spirits, including a belief in 'messengers of the gods', powerful angelic forces mediated between gods and humans. They also believed that each person had a 'ghost', the equivalent of a 'guardian angel' and this entity remained a constant companion for a person throughout their entire life.

Excavations of ancient Sumerian homes have revealed altars that seem to be dedicated to guardian angels, along with stone engravings and temple wall paintings of human figures with wings. No doubt these Sumerian ideas influenced cross-pollination for the development of Egyptian theology as well.

In the year 2335 BCE the Akkadian tribes conquered the Sumerians, who adopted the cosmological concept of angels developing the idea of an entire body of angels divided into groupings serving each of the many Semitic gods, and further subdividing these groups into vertical 'ranked' hierarchies. This notion continued in Zoroastrianism, a religion that is still relatively unknown in the West.

To the Zoroastrians the seven divine beings were symbolized by the planets; Sun, Moon, Mars, Mercury, Jupiter, Venus and Saturn; rotating luminaries that could be seen by the naked eye in the skies at night. These divine beings were not just governing the heavens, but also assigned to a day of the week.

Archangels may have links with the Zoroastrian term 'Amesha Spenta' referring to divine sparks or seven divine beings who were attendants to Ahura Mazda god of fire, the Supreme Universal Lord.

Fire represents the symbol of divine life and is the sacred symbol most reverenced by the Zoroastrians of today.

Fire is confirmed to be the most caring of all the spiritual intelligences or archangels, and is regarded as the 'friendliest'.

Coming down from Ahura Mazda, fire is acquainted with all heavenly secrets.

In every religion, fire has been the symbol of the Supreme Creator. Brahman is fire in Hinduism. The Jews worship their God as a pillar of fire and Christians declare that their God is a consuming fire.

It was from Zoroastrianism that Jews received for the first time the concept of heaven and hell, of angels and archangels, of the resurrection and the last day of judgement.

These have laid the foundation to the doctrines of Christianity and Islam. Throughout these cultures and beyond, to the present-day, images of beings with wings, we know as angels, can be found the world over.

Angels have many titles; Indian yogis refer to angels as 'Himalayan masters'; theosophists call them 'devas'; spiritualist's refer to them as 'helpers', 'the gatekeeper' and 'guides', whilst others talk about the 'over self' or 'higher consciousness'. The Hebrew word is 'mal'akh', translated as 'messenger' or 'one going' or 'one sent'.

Our word 'angel' comes from the Greek 'angelos'. The origins suggest a being responsible for carrying messages between the human world and some other realm or realms of existence, someone who is a mediator between 'down here' and 'up there'.

It is well documented throughout the Bible and other Holy works that winged beings represent a body of spirits who acted as intermediaries between God and man and since very early time's man has sought to communicate with these higher powers.

During the medieval age man would call upon the services of a Magus, often known as 'in the service of God'. These Magi were so important they were treated with 'royal status' and so revered a priest with special writing skills was assigned to work with them in order to gain wisdom that only the angels could provide.

Do you think this is the case – the Medieval Magus generally had to keep his work hidden due to concerns over persecution? Even Johannes Dee (Philosopher, scientist and magician and personal astrologer to Queen Elizabeth 1ˢᵗ) had to be very wary and focus on astrology and less challenging material publicly.

As one cannot speak in the verbal sense directly to God, the belief was that via the angels, the words of the Magus would be heard. The scribe would record detailed information of all that the Magus had performed and said, including the results of his work. The writings were catalogued and then bound into manuscripts called 'grimoires'. These manuscripts contained incredibly powerful conjurations and invocations designed solely to summon angels, demons, or other spirits.

It was noted that the Magus used particular objects in his ritual of invoking and conjuring the angels. The first to be mentioned is candles. Some of us light candles for the sheer pleasure of watching the flickering flame. In medieval times the Magus would select a special candle, thoroughly cleanse it of negativity and charge it with his highest intentions, by incising the sides of the candle with sigils. He would then set about invoking a conjuration to summon the angel either to ask a favour or gain particular knowledge. It is stated in some grimoires that not only did the angel manifest in the smoke of the candle but actually spoke divine words to the Magus.

'I implore Thee, O Holy Adonay, Amy, Horta, Vegadoro, Ysion, Ysesy, and by all They Holy Names, and by all Thine Angels, Archangels, and Powers, Dominations, and virtues, and by Thy Name with which King Solomon did bind up the devils and shut them up, Ethrack, Evanher, Agla, Goth, Joth, Othie, Venock, Nabrat, and by all Thy Holy Names which are written in this book, and by virtue of them all, that Thou enable me to congregate all Thy spirits, that they may give me true answers to all my demands.' *The Secret Grimoire of Turiel* Translated from the Latin version of 1518 – author unknown.

The scholar and mystic Dr. Johannes Dee owned a copy of *De Originibus*. The sections that particularly interested him related to an Ethiopian priest's statement that this book contained Enoch's own record of the language God had taught Adam to use to name the beasts and the birds. Dr Dee's reaction was immediately to ask the Archangel Uri'el about the *Book of Soyga*, a tome very precious to him.

Dee employed the talents of the medium Sir Edward Talbot later known as Edward Kelley, a mysterious figure who entered Dr Dee's life. His first question to Uri'el, communicated by Talbot was: 'Is my *Book of Soyga* of any excellency?' he asked.

> 'That book was revealed to Adam in paradise by the
> Angels of God,' Uri'el replied.'
>
> *The Queen's Conjuror* Benjamin Woolley.

Another object a Magus would use is incense, employed in the same way as a candle, providing the angel with the vehicle of 'smoke' to enable it to materialize in form. Incense has been used since ancient times to attract the attention of spiritual creatures, and also as a vessel for taking prayer to the heavens.

Angels love aroma and colour. Have you often wondered why sometimes you may smell the fragrance of lilies and automatically look for someone holding flowers? Next time this happens, thank the angelic force as it could very well be the archangel Gabri'el making his presence felt.

Although candles and incense have been used by different people, different religions, and in different time periods, one thing is certain, they have withstood the test of time. In this modern age most of us use candles in the same way, but by varying degrees.

One might light a candle to invoke health for a loved one who is ill, or for the wellbeing of their family and friends. Some may use them for the energies they possess in them. For example when invoking Mikh'ael you would use an orange or red candle. Combine that with the aroma of incense for protection and your candle draws even more energy in itself. Saying your invocation whilst lighting your candle makes your intentions loud and clear for all the angelic beings to hear.

Burning incense not only helps draw the spirits closer to you, but also aids relaxation and opens one's mind. The energies that incense holds are just as strong as the candle. By explaining angelic magic in this way casts off the fear and evil associated with it. You could add prayers/hymns to attract their attention, also include talismans as part of this ritual.

There are generally two ways in which believers make contact with Angels, either by evocation or invocation.

Evocations are particular spells that use a selection of different tools or objects that might include: incense, candles, books, knives and circles drawn upon the floor. However, the workings may vary depending on the type of spell being used. As mentioned, incense is one of the more frequently used tools as it serves as a vehicle in which the angel manifests. They are also known to appear in a crystal ball, magic mirror or bowl of water.

Invocations are very similar to evocations, but there is one main difference; the one trying to summon the angel endeavours to persuade him to enter their body as opposed to physically appearing. This is so they can communicate with them. Even though the latter is considered more dangerous, it is still regarded as an easier thing to do.

As not all of us have access to the ancient grimoires, I decided to combine magical workings using pathworking and invocations.

By using the Angelic Language of Dr. Johannas Dee we will endeavour to recreate the link between man and the angelic realm. The intention is to commune with angels such as Mikh'ael, Gabri'el and Sama'el through to Rapha'el, Zadki'el, Ana'el, Cassi'el and Uri'el. Under the guidance of Enoch we will be transported to the fields of the fallen ones, the Irim, known as the Grigori and be privy to the catastrophic results as half-breeds emerged - the Nephilim.

Each chapter is accompanied by a legend explaining the meaning and purpose behind each archangel, but please do not look upon the words as empty verbalism; they are designed to enhance and enrich our lives as we enter into the realm of each winged being. The invocations themselves are elegant, powerful and to the point. I have tried not to fall into the trap by using flowery language.

The feeling throughout is, that whilst opening up to the realms of the Angels and calling them in, one is always grounded.

Although the senses are heightened, engendered within are emotions of deep spiritual calm, together with connection the angel and the powers of the universe.

All pathworkings have a beginning, middle and an end and your journeys will commence in front of an Angel Hair quartz crystal door forming an entrance through which you can leave your world behind. This door should be constructed with love and care. Recognize each carved and faceted angle. Marvel at the smoky golden brown strands tipped with red sparks of colour as if spirits dance within. Visualise a brilliant shaft of light pass through it, as you gently touch the door's surface, listen to words ring out; 'All man is divine'.

Not only will you be going on a pathworking, but a journey into the centre of the Angelic realm. As you enter, learn to tune and energise your being as you are drawn in. Envisage this crystal doorway each time you go on your journey, it will be your safeguard.

As the Angelic forces present themselves to you, be guided by them and they will impart to you the secrets and mysteries that lay within their dominion. Remember they are real and powerful energies, so approach them with respect and you will find pathways open up before you. Many of the Angels you may come to love with all your heart, whilst others …

On your second journey, Path to Mikh'ael, your personal magical name will be revealed to you. This name you will use throughout all your pathworkings and will be known solely by you. Reveal it to no one else, as it is said: 'By revealing your secret name gives others power over you'.

With all your pathworking journeys, you will need a guide – I have chosen Luc'ifer, as he was the most beloved of God. Many of you may baulk at the thought of such an angelic being accompany you, having been swayed by stories about him. You may know him as the rebellious angel who was cast out of paradise because he made claims on taking over heaven and the Throne of God. He is, by the way, the first creature of God, but termed the 'devil' by impostors and the ignorant. The intellectual Luc'ifer personifies the spirit of intelligence and love; the Holy

Spirit, while the physical Luc'ifer is the great agent of universal magnetism. This agent is infinite light, and as you traverse the many paths, the great Luc'ifer of Nature will be the perfect mediator between matter and spirit. He will prove more than a guide; he will be your companion. Therefore, do not judge this son of the morning, for he was after all the most favoured and most loved by God, perhaps throughout your journeys, he may relate his story to you.

Your journey will end much as you began; returning to the mundane world through the portal, and hearing the crystal door close behind you. It is of paramount importance to hear that door close. It must be pointed out that many problems can occur if that door is not properly closed. It is just commonsense and makes for good psychic hygiene. Doorways have been opened both mentally and on the astral plane, and you need to ensure nothing comes through which is going to negatively affect either you, or your environment.

This book explores and explains the relationship between the higher powers, and provides ways for you to communicate with the teaching angels relating to the various planets. It must be pointed out that Mars, Saturn and Uranus have undeservedly been regarded as evil planets and are constantly blamed for many of the difficulties, troubles and sorrows in life. However, the angelic forces relating to these planets are sent to guide and support us. This underlying support helps us overcome misfortunes and engenders learning – imagine a life without errors - we would make no progress at all, and would remain undeveloped beings.

It has been said that life on Earth is a school; the initiates are in the classroom whilst others remain in the playground! Once we have learned the lessons taught by Mars, Saturn and Uranus the aspects we consider bad, cease to affect us.

If there were only good aspects in our lives, we would be human cabbages, incapable of understanding the troubles of others, and having no experience of suffering ourselves - for what humanity has never known, humanity cannot understand.

Hence, we must learn to strive upward, always aspiring to win a soul that elevates us above the animals.

After which time, proceeding by degrees and mastering the planetary forces and effects, each of us will be reabsorbed into the Supreme Creator, from whence to be transformed as Angels, whereby reincarnation in human form will cease. The angelic role would be to teach the inhabitants of the new universes, which are being created all the time. Ours is but one of many worlds, our universe but one of many magical others. Such is the Master Plan of the Grand Architect of the universe – The Creator.

The more we learn, the more the angelic forces help us upwards, and less effect the planets have to affect us. We become masters of our own fate, and no longer victims of it.

Combining pathworking and invocation, one remains focused, and is able to create a vibrant and potent two-way flow with the angel to be invoked, thereby opening a channel smoothly rather than using force. Many symbols will be presented to you throughout your pathworkings, such as animals, insects, flowers and trees. Look upon these symbols as signposts that may very well embed themselves subliminally upon your psyche, only to be recalled as an indication that the angelic force has recognized your plea. But be warned! Angelic magic is powerful and certain angels take longer to fulfil a request and before you realize, you may have asked for something that you no longer need.

Before reading any further, I must stress that angelic magic is a very serious practice, and should not be entered into lightly!

Author's Note

The books on angels are to numerous to count; there are the heavy magickal tomes that are so impossible to navigate the readers are forced to close the covers in defeat, whilst others are just so shallow they only serve to give the reader a false view of these ancient winged beings.

Through *Walking with Angels* I have endeavoured to open up the experience of communicating with the winged beings either by simply writing a letter on their special day and time, or an even more direct contact through a pathworking. In my own way, I am attempting to speak, on behalf of the angels.

I, like all magicians have my own method when it comes to carrying out a working, and this will be evident in the nine paths. I have used a particular approach to each angel; a careful use of symbols that will subliminally impact on the reader, use of the angelic language, and the introduction of the Seal of Truth, or the Sigilum dei Aemeth.

I wanted to get away from the 'flat earth' principle and for this reason I broke the sigil up into bite size chunks providing seven approaches towards the divine experience, man is looking for. Personally, this is one of the many sigils that for me *had* to be dissected and used in stages. Master magicians will probably disagree, but it rests with the readers who will I hope, work the sigil and re-find the true meaning.

My understanding of the Sigilum dei Aemeth is as follows:

At the dawning of eternity, the innermost universe was already in existence and the billion perfect worlds surrounding what we understand as Heaven are not a creation of time, as these perfect worlds existed before time. These worlds, although were composed of the basic life patterns that are replicated on the evolutionary worlds, were replete. Each one of these worlds is overflowing with endless discoveries.

The heavenly worlds are arranged in seven levels all leading in stages towards Paradise, all looked on, by the angelic realm, the children of the Archangels, Sons and the Daughters and the Sons of the Sons, and Daughters of the Daughters.

As an aspirant alights at the edge and outermost rim, it is here the personal training begins. When they traverse these other realms, it is hoped they become spiritually, intellectually, and philosophically perfected. The investment in our extensive training is a reminder of the promise we have come to trust, as each of us is of supreme value to the Creator.

Travelling the Paths, we learn as we visit each realm, from the first step to the seventh; Heaven. We can only marvel at theses other worlds as they are beyond anything we could imagine on our journey via the planets and beyond through the super-universe.

When writing the pathworkings, I never dreamed of what would begin to unfold. The twists and turns of the angels revealed things I could never have known. It is not another world it is another realm beyond our world.

Although we will travel meta-physically to the planets, when it is all said and done, the angelic dominion is still shrouded in mystery.

Practical Matters

There is, however, a practical side of magical work that includes:

-- ritual washing

-- wearing of white clothes

-- offering of incense

-- offering of water, and drink

-- charging an appropriate stone or crystal

Think about the matter of your own space and time. Most of us do not have much of either. Few of us have spare rooms where we can isolate ourselves for meditation or invocation, and many of us have to be discreet in our activities. Endeavour to keep a realistic timetable, and keep to it, especially when working angelic magic as each has his time and specific day. This will help build discipline. Learn to be discreet in your activities; we may live in freer times, but the spectre of religious prejudice is still an issue to contend with. People tend to fear and distrust what they do not understand, so be sensible and do not make life difficult for yourself. Know when to open up and when to remain silent. Over time, you will learn to cultivate the qualities of discretion and discrimination. It is as much about training the mind and the body as it is about learning the practical skills of magical work.

For less experienced

Experienced practitioners may wish to skip this section and begin directly with the pathworkings. As for the beginner, what might you do in preparation?

Firstly, consider your motives for deciding to read this book. What do you wish to gain from it? How will you use the knowledge contained within it? Once that is clear in your mind, you have a foundation to build the Temple of the Self upon. Our spiritual journey can start in the most mundane of ways!

Research the angels – how they affected people, culture, society, and religion.

Changes will inevitably occur when the inner levels are contacted – issues that have laid buried deep within your subconscious will begin to stir and make inroads into your conscious mind. Your emotions will be stirred, in ways not to your liking, but like any situation in life we have to face them. Self-honesty is a difficult thing, as is self-acceptance – warts and all. A well balanced, healthy inner state of being will equip you with the skills you need to cope with all that life can throw at you. Above all, be gentle with yourself and do not set unrealistic goals.

What might you need? I suggest you wear a plain white robe made from natural material such as cotton or linen for example; wearing white shows that you are ritually pure. You can either choose to buy it or make it yourself. But, it must be your robe - no one else must be allowed to wear it. Putting on that robe symbolizes that you are putting aside the mundane world and stepping into the world of the spirit. The Internet is a good resource to use in search of further information. For example, Servants of the Light Mystery School (S.O.L.) has information on its website regarding the making of robes and cloaks. (www.servantsofthelight.org)

As you will be working with numerous different Angels, I suggest you wear a coloured sash or cord corresponding to a particular angel (see Angel Chart). A visit to your local department store may be useful; they can be a good source of materials for your magical wardrobe.

Cleansing

Before doing any magickal work I always recommend to people to take a shower, or preferably a long, hot soaking bath. One tradition is to bless salt, and mix it into the water; this exorcises the water of any energy's other than cleansing ones.

You may want to make up a small sachet of mixed crushed herbs and drop them into the bath so that you can breathe in their odours while you bathe.

Play soothing music on a recorder, burn appropriate incense, light a candle, or add any other elements you like that will reinforce two primary ideas: 1) getting rid of all previous thoughts and obsessions, and 2) beginning to focus on the energies to be worked with in the upcoming rite.

When you get out of the shower/bath put on your white robe and without letting your mind drift too far into other topics, go straight to the place where you will be doing your magical work.

Angelic altar and tools

There is no set rule for creating an altar in your home, as the altar is very much a unique reflection of you and your inner self. It must be stressed the importance of cleansing and charging each item that will be placed on your altar, to the particular energies for which they are intended.

It is quite simple to set up a basic altar, and this can range from the top of a dresser to a small table or a lockable box in which you can store your robe and other ritual equipment. The piece of furniture used as the altar needs to be cleansed by wiping it thoroughly with a solution of salt and water, making sure that it is dried properly afterwards.

You will need a pair of candlesticks, a supply of candles and a piece of natural fabric that serves as an altar cloth. An alternative to candles are T-lights or a small lamp.

If you wish to have an altar cloth and if you are handy with a needle and thread you could embroider a compass and the four points. Or perhaps you could draw the symbol on white cloth using colour felt-tip pens. Remember, it is the intention that counts, not your artistic ability. Angelic forces recognize your sincerity and will hear your call.

As mentioned, apart from colour, angels love aroma, so you may want to use an incense burner. A word of precaution; charcoal gets very hot, and stays that way for a long time, so a metal bowl containing charcoal can scorch a table, and a glass bowl will crack with the heat. I therefore suggest one made of earthenware. To keep the base of the bowl cool, put a layer of sand about one inch thick in the bottom of the vessel, then place the prepared charcoal on the sand. For further protection of surfaces, always place the incense burner on an insulated or fireproof mat or trivet.

When using incense, it is normal for the ingredients in the incense to give off large amounts of smoke. We all know that excessive exposure to smoke, in all its forms, is not good for the health, especially when used in a confined space. Billowing smoke may look dramatic, but will not make an impression on the divine energies you are working with. So, ensure your place of magical working is well ventilated as much as possible. Also ensure that you only purchase a non-combustible type of incense, from a reputable supplier who only uses 100% natural ingredients.

Remember that a small amount of incense goes a long way. Think of the size of a salt spoon, just one scoop of incense may be sufficient for your invocation, especially in a small room.

If you are not happy using incense, then don't. Working in a smoke-filled atmosphere is not recommended, as it will penetrate a house or flat.

Some people cannot tolerate this so you may want to consider using an oil vaporizer instead. The candle goes under the bowl that contains water, followed by a few drops of scented oil. This will perfume a room without smoke to worry other people. It is also less of a health and fire risk.

For those who cannot burn incense or use an oil vaporizer, use essential oil. The 'pleasing smell' is what is needed. Always put a little of the oil on your skin to test sensitivity before using it during a particular ceremony. The advice given is not meant to be full, conclusive or based on any scientific or practical research, it is meant to make you aware that the use of some materials may have harmful effects, and therefore caution is advised at all times. For your oil fragrances, Woods Health Products has an excellent range (www.woodshealth.com/)

As the angels have particular stones appropriated to them, you may wish to place one on your altar to be charged during your pathworking. Try Angel Additions, the only authorised worldwide stockist of crystals charged by the acclaimed author Judy Hall, www.angeladditions.co.uk. Contact them to receive a stone specially attuned to you and your angel.

The Angel

You might want a statuette or picture of the angel with whom you are seeking contact and there are many about, but buying all of them would be a costly business. Be practical and realistic in your expectations, and if your budget is constrained a picture of the angel can serve as a focus for your worship just as well. In fact the angel is present regardless of whether it is in the form of an illustration or an actual statuette. Remember, it is the sincerity of your feelings not the depth of your wallet that is important here.

Meditation

Don't be afraid of rehearsing. Meditation does not come easily to many people. The greatest magicians and high priests have all had to practise before they became legendary figures. They all trained and sweated and worked to achieve magnificent results. Be realistic about your goals, pace your self and learn to 'see' from different viewpoints, for truth can be multi-layered.

How often should a pathworking be done? For beginners, one working per week is sufficient. This form of magical work is not meant to take over your life, and as with everything else, should be done in moderation.

The workings will impact upon your inner and outer worlds, profoundly in the case of certain angels, so cultivate patience. A seedling tended with care, love and patience soon develops into a strong and healthy plant, just like the developing divine consciousness.

No two pathworkings are alike in their approach to this practice, so some method of monitoring is suggested. It may be useful to keep a diary of your working, as over time you are able to chart your progress, keep methods that work, and amend or discard those that don't. A diary will also be a valuable record of the development of your magical personality.

Apart from pathworking and invocation, you may wish to correspond with each Angel using sacred scripts. Since man has held belief in angels, he has also sought help and harness their powers for his own ends.

We have taken a brief look at the practical side of pathworking; now let us consider the more spiritual side of working with the Angelic Realm as we begin our pathworking.

1
Archangel Luc'ifer
'Carrier of the Light'

Legend

The word 'Luc'ifer' is derived from two Latin words: Lux = light + ferrous – to bear or carry. Thus the name 'Luc'ifer' means: Light-bearer, Light Bringer or Carrier of Light.

The name 'Luc'ifer' is mentioned only once in the Bible. Any other mention is with other names, such as Satan, Devil, or Dragon. He is often associated with the ancient Egyptian god Set, the King of Babylon and Prometheus. Yet, all readers and believers, and many non-believers, think of Luc'ifer as a fallen angel who turned against God and paid for it by being banished from heaven. Other similar stories are told in the Bible, connecting Luc'ifer as the being that has forever plagued the world with evil.

If asked who Luc'ifer is, the average person in the street will tell you some story about him being a disobedient angel who was cast out of heaven because he wanted to take over the 'Throne of God'.

However the Bible doesn't actually say that, other than a Luc'ifer character being anything other than a shining planet or morning star that everyone can see with his or her own eyes if they know when and where to look.

The narrative entails a hypothetical 'War in Heaven'. Despite not being able to point to some actual 'Heaven' where the war is taking place, or took place, or even to some 'Hell' where the imaginary Luc'ifer character is currently chained up, many people seem to believe this and take it seriously.

Luc'ifer is still alive and well, according to most Christians, which makes sense, since everyone can actually see the planet Venus/Luc'ifer shining in the heavens.

Earlier versions of the Bible do not use the word Luc'ifer, but use 'morning star' or 'star of dawn'.

As already mentioned, 'Luc'ifer' is not an English word, but a Latin word. The question is: who gave the world this Latin name?

The Bible does not name the devil as Luc'ifer. The use of this name in reference to the devil originates from an interpretation of Isaiah 14:3-20, a passage that does not speak of any 'fallen angel' but of the defeat of a particular Babylonian King, to who it gives a title that refers to what in English is called the Day Star or Morning Star (in Latin, *Luc'ifer*). In 2 Peter 1:19 and elsewhere, the same Latin word *Luc'ifer* is used to refer to the Morning Star, with no relation to the devil.

It is only in New Testament times that the Latin word *Luc'ifer* was used as a name for the devil. This name occurred both in religious writing and in fiction, especially when referring to Luc'ifer's fall from Heaven.

In the King James Version and New King James Version, which are both relative newcomers as far as Bible translations go, Isaiah 14:12-16 mentions Luc'ifer only once by name and tells his story:

> 'How art thou fallen from heaven, O Luc'ifer, son of the morning! How art thou cut down to the ground, which didst weaken the nations! For thou hast said in thine heart, I will ascend into heaven, I will exalt my throne above the stars of God: I will sit also upon the mount of the congregation, in the sides to the north: I will ascend above the heights of the clouds: I will be like the Most High.'

Later, in Ezeki'el, the story is repeated, with God speaking all that he will do to the one who opposes him. This being is again Luc'ifer, and the reader is given a specific physical description of Luc'ifer that makes one see him as the angel we believe him to be. Just as for us the Creator's plans for Luc'ifer were for good and not evil. He was created as the minister of music in heaven.

Ezeki'el 28:13-14 'You were in Eden, the Garden of God; every precious stone was your covering: The sardius, topaz and diamond, beryl, onyx, and Jasper, sapphire, turquoise, and emerald with gold. The workmanship of your timbrels and pipes was prepared for you on the day you were created. You were anointed cherub who covers; I established you; you were on the holy mountain of God; you walked back and forth in the midst of fiery stones.'

Ezeki'el 28:14 says: *'Thou art the anointed cherub that covereth'*, meaning he is the angel that protects God.

Ezeki'el 28:17 reads, *'Thine heart was lifted up because of thy beauty: thou has corrupted thy wisdom by reason of they brightness'*, tells the reader that Luc'ifer was a beautiful angel with a large, vain, ego. However, it is Ezeki'el 28:13 that makes one question Luc'ifer's connection with music:

> 'The workmanship of they tabrets and of they pipes was prepared in thee in the day that thou wast created.'

Luc'ifer was a beautiful angel covered in musical instruments so he could sing the praises of God. But, he denied God and became Satan, the evil that plagues us and tempts us? It is the description of this evil that makes one question, if Luc'ifer was the angel of music then we should consider music evil and corrupting.

First version

Luc'ifer had been highly exalted, and knew that angels obeyed his command without question; after all, he was the favourite in heaven and glorified in his superiority. Luc'ifer had been near the Great Creator from the beginning, and the ceaseless beams of glorious light enshrouding the eternal One had shone especially upon Luc'ifer. But pride, the gravest of the seven deadly sins eventually led to the expulsion from Heaven of particular beings, up to and including the highest orders of angels.

Luc'ifer was the first and most powerful angel to be created, and due to this, succumbed to pride and arrogance. He was gifted in intelligence, radiance, beauty and authority unmatched among all of the angels in Heaven and was second in magnificence only to the Creator Himself.

Regrettably, Luc'ifer became ambitious and egotistical, finally deciding to demonstrate his power by elevating his throne to the height of that of the Creator's.

Other angels did not agree with Luc'ifer's plan; for a lower being to symbolically become the equal of the Creator was abhorrent to them, and hence Luc'ifer was instantly hurled out of Heaven.

There are a numerous beliefs about fallen angels, and much focus on matters of lust, pride, free will, or the air of mystery surrounding the acts of God.

An act by the God of creation was forecast as resulting in multiple outcomes, with each of these three doctrines that were traits held by certain angels. These fallen angels foresaw impending doom. In one entity, that is both omnipotent and omnipresent, who gives certain ideas to humanity and expects only one right way to live - by universal morals, ethics and faith. However, given the doctrine of free will, each one of these ideas leads one to speculate on the basis of duality of right and wrong, good and evil, and heaven and hell.

Second version

After the creation of mankind, the Creator forgot his previous mandate and ordered the angels to bow down before the new figure; man. But Luc'ifer refused; firstly because he could not forget his first mandate, and second and most important of all, he would bow to his beloved Creator only! When the other angels saw this, they regarded Luc'ifer as rebellious, and expelled him from Heaven. Those who believe in this version do not regard Luc'ifer or the fallen angels to be demons, since they did not rebel against the Creator by refusing his mandate, but believed that creatures should bow before only the Creator, and no one else.

Magical Intentions: Invoking the power of light through darkness. Luc'ifer sustains good marital relations and is to be sought in matters of love, peace and harmony, also for creating beautiful things. He may raise storms. Seek him out for advice about hidden as well as spiritual matters.

Negative aspects: Vanity and false pride

Positive aspects: Loyalty, devotion, unconditional love

Above all other angels, Luc'ifer is known to be the great angel of beauty and elegance, Angel of Venus who rules two signs of the zodiac, Libra (positive) and Taurus  (negative). Colours representative of Luc'ifer are: black, red, and gold.

Throughout the pathworking many signs and symbolic forms will be revealed to you and it is important that you remember them, especially if you intend writing letters of petition.

When writing to this angel, first draw his four symbols, write 'To Archangel Luc'ifer' followed by the letter of request, all of which is written in Passing the Rivers Script and finally sign your secret name.

The letter must be written on a Friday at the appointed hour (see chart), using white paper and blue ink for Taurus, and pink paper and red ink for Libra. The letter is kept for a lunar month (twenty eight days) and on the fourth Friday it is burnt.

Luc'ifer may use one or several of the signs during the course of the twenty-eight days, but one sign is enough to assume your request has been granted.

If you receive no sign from him, your request is refused. Magical help is not intended to take the place of your own efforts.

Magical letters can be written to any of the Ruling Angels but only on matters He rules, and on His day, you need to invoke or banish.

Do not complicate this system beyond what is given, as the letter is sufficient. Simplicity is the beauty of this art, the Voice of

Angels is not a ritual, add the knowledge to what you already have and don't confuse systems.

'May the Archangel Luc'ifer grant and bless your request'

Path to Archangel Luc'ifer

What you will need:
Oil of frankincense, incense, charcoal, goblet of wine/beer, fruit juice or water, two candles; one red and one black, a statue or picture of the angel (optional but very useful).

Preparation:
Don your white robe and tie a gold and black cord around your waist. This will be in respect for the Angel you will be working with. Anoint wrists, temples and throat with oil of frankincense. Light candles. Prepare charcoal and add incense as required. Fill goblet with liquid and raise it in salutation to the angels and place it back on your altar.

Sit comfortably in an upright chair and inhale very slowly and deeply. You are not just inhaling air, but joy, serenity, strength, vitality, courage, and whichever positive quality you want to affirm. Imagine the breath filling not only your lungs, but also the whole body – starting from the feet and culminating at a point between the eyebrows.

As you exhale not only do you expel carbon dioxide from your system, but also mental and emotional impurities such as weakness, discouragement and despair. Feel the intimate connection between the mind and the breath. Feel the flow of energy around your body as you prepare for your ritual working.

Say the temple prayer to the angels:

I call upon thy sacred name

Of the being that has been with me

Since the beginning of beginnings.

As I gaze upwards,

May I behold thy beauty and thy splendour unto eternity,

Time without end.

Build your gate with love and care; visualise Angel Hair quartz crystal the colour of citrine pushing up through the earth, towering above your head and disappearing into the heavens. Visualise a brilliant shaft of light pass through it. Marvel at the smoky golden brown strands tipped with red sparks of colour as spirits dance within. Feel the warmth of sunbeams as you pass through the gleaming portal. Inner voices ring out: 'All man is Divine' – feel the words within your heart.

The skies are open for you - and the endless expanse of the universe is beyond. But not a universe of stars as you would imagine; this is a universe-field that is dragging angelic forces towards you. From within this force is a being that has travelled through space and time to be with you.

'Release me!'

You look around as the voice echoes in your head.

Fear suddenly grips you as you realize that you are standing on a ten-edged crystal platform – and beneath it is the great abyss. The fathomless void makes you want to look down – *Don't* be tempted!

Materializing in front of you is a golden cage in the shape of a three-sided pyramid, the top is encrusted with hundreds of garnet seals; each with a sigil embedded in it. Inside is a crouching youth who extends his arm through the bars towards you. Hastily you step back and for a split second you want to escape back to your mundane world.

'Break the seals that bind me!' the youth pleads.

'You are the special one I have been waiting for. Please don't leave me here caged. I am Luc'ifer 'Most beloved of God'. I beg you, set me free,'

Release Luc'ifer? You stand mesmerized looking into his beseeching eyes, then at his outstretched hand. Without thinking, you touch his fingers. The contact explodes the seals away from the cage, shattering them into millions of fragments that fall slowly about you like drops of blood. The bars spin away forming a golden corona providing an opening for Luc'ifer to step through.

Luc'ifer is free! He stands beside you tossing back his shoulder-length blonde curly hair, stretches his arms and takes a long deep breath. His eyes shine forth like amber orbs, he is beautiful. Happiness and exhilaration lights his face, his full lips curve into a smile. His forehead is high and broad, showing a powerful intellect.

He wears a simple black linen robe edged in plaited gold braid, around his neck suspended from a gold chain hangs the nine jewel-encrusted Ephod, his feet are bare. You gaze in wonder at this fabulous jewel; sardius, topaz, carbuncle, emerald, sapphire, diamond, ligure, white agate and amethyst; each stone pulsates its own energy. From his back delicate leather-like wings gently unfold. Luc'ifer smiles and turns away from you walking clockwise round the perimeter of the platform tracing a line through the air with his left hand; and touching the sardius stone on the Ephod, he whispers an invocation.

The atmosphere shimmers around you as ten crystal walls erupt from the abyss and tower above.

Emblazoned on one of the first cell wall is his signature; Archangel Luc'ifer.

Luc'ifer

lu – CEE-FA

Commit it to memory. This symbol is charged, look at each mark and take it within. Around your feet an opaque layer of highly reflective clouds of sulphuric acid form. The atmosphere is dense consisting of mostly carbon dioxide. This is Venus; it doesn't appear to have any organic life to absorb it in biomass. When Venus was younger it is believed to have possessed Earth-like oceans, but these evaporated as the temperature rose. The crystal wall melts away.

You are standing on the Sixth Foundation of Heaven; an opaque opalescent glow is all around you. Luc'ifer strides forward and gestures for you to follow him.

Uncertainty makes you hesitate, but a voice whispers: 'Let go of your fear, it is but an opening into other states of being.' In your heart you know the truth of that statement. Look at him Pilgrim; trust him, as he will be your guide throughout your journeys.

You walk between two towering columns of red sardius stone. Luc'ifer says:

'Know this Pilgrim; these very columns symbolize the foundation of heaven. Once the universe was filled with red hot bodies of matter, and to remind us, the Great Creator encapsulated part of heaven in them.' Luc'ifer lovingly touches the columns that transmit a rosy glow that bathes your body.

'I pray thee Archangel Luc'ifer, who art thou?'

Luc'ifer stands tall; his magnificent leather-like wings fold and unfold sending a myriad of changing colours through the atmosphere.

'In the heart of darkness, my time began.

With wings of divine light I greet the dawn.

Pilgrim, I am the Son of the Morning,

I am born out of the eclipse of fire.

I am the last, proud star shining from within the firmament

Before obliterating the light of the daystar.

I teach wisdom and all things in moderation,

So that the brightness of truth is not overwhelming.'

You look at him with uncertainty. Much darkness has entered the world of humans, souls drowning in a sea of greed and lost in ignorance. He reads your mind.

'Pilgrim, why are you uncomfortable with the thought that I have abandoned you?

How low have I sunk in your estimation?

To know and embrace me is to know and embrace your self,

And fathom your inner most depths that you guard and keep hidden.'

How well he knows you Pilgrim. Luc'ifer continues:

'I can wait for an eternity.

Eventually you will want to know what light I bring.'

Look around you Pilgrim, reach out and touch what IS. Luc'ifer continues:

'The Absolute Realm is composed of Eternity, Awareness and Infinity. These three go beyond all things and come before all else. They are the source of all beginnings. They are the foundations and the sustaining of all. Even before the beginning, there was, and is, and always shall be, the Absolute Realm.'

Luc'ifer takes a deep breath, and extending his hands into the heavens above, says:

'May all realities and planes of existence emanate from the Absolute Realm. And thus pouring forth from the Absolute Realm is the love and the divine wisdom of the Great Creator toward all of his creation. I have much to show you.'

An Infinite expanse of patterns and light swirl about you expanding into three dimensions like an explosion of thoughts. Overwhelming joy and delight fills you as you experience the first simple steps of the Creators universe. Out of the darkness of nothing a tiny spark appears. Within the space form beautiful intricate patterns of white lines, white circles that curl, all intertwined like visual music. A sob rises within you as you watch Luc'ifer orchestrating from memory the entire spectacle with his very breath. He smiles, and in a voice, full of pride, he says:

'Pilgrim, you see the very beginnings of the Dreams of the Creator and of the Realm of Chaos.'

Luc'ifer pauses, and looks into the distance, saying:

'I experienced the time when the Great Creator first dreamed. It was like a cup of dreams flowing over like a river overflowing its banks. In an instant the Creator dreamed an infinity of dreams that multiplied by infinity for an Eternity creating all that is possible in one momentous Now!

This was the Realm of Chaos. Outside the Absolute Realm the Creator began the first realities built on dimensions and textures. He created a reflection of his awareness and gave the reflection purpose. Then, He created beings of beauty and intellect with a sense of self. He gave them permanent independence, and free will. He created Us, the Angels.'

You hear the flapping of leather-like wings about you, and cries of disdain, but Luc'ifer ignores these and continues:

'At the time of our creation our design and purpose is set for eternity. Our Maker created us to share the dream and help Him guide the dream.

The Creator sent Independent Awareness into His Infinities, and the Now was filled with millions of Angels who observed the wonders of His creation, but not yet seen. The Creator used Us to apply His will in all that he had created.'

Luc'ifer pauses, looking thoughtful, and says:

'We began our existence with no memory. So, the Creator fashioned independent minds with Awareness. That which is observed by the created becomes part of what we call the past, and that which is yet unobserved is what we call the future. Pilgrim, for the first time from the beginning of the *first* Angel, past and future had meaning. Imagine my joy?'

'Our Maker created three Archangels; my brother Mikh'ael, brother Gabri'el, and me to rule over the cherubim and angels, and to oversee the government of the Creator throughout the Angelic Realm. We were perfect in His making and had freedom to wander wherever we pleased.'

'Mikh'ael served Eternity, Gabri'el served Awareness and I served Infinity.

'But out of all my brothers, it was me the Great Creator chose.'

Why? You ask yourself, Luc'ifer reads your mind, and answers:

'Because I have the greatest light and brilliance and resemble the brightest star of all.'

His words are unreal, magical, and full of ethereal colours that surround you making you feel strangely purified. Luc'ifer smiles, and continues.

'I pleased Him because I knew how to search the Infinities for the jewels of reality. Although my brothers became instruments of Awareness, peering into the Infinite possibilities and manifesting realities created, it was I, Luc'ifer who brought the beauty before the throne of the Eternal. It was *my* sharp and keen awareness that continued to find much splendour hidden in the infinite possibilities the Creator had set into motion.'

Millions of stars fall about you, each one touching you delicately making your skin tingle with pleasure. The beauty is so magnificent the angels shout for joy. The spell thrown over you is not so much a spell woven of details, but a spell woven of divine uniformity.

Pilgrim you are witnessing the time when the Great Creator brings forth the greatest jewel of all. The creation of the Infinities containing the Physical Realm where now the possibility of life exists. For it is in this new and beautiful expanse, we call the heavens, that the Creator has placed a new and wonderful jewel. A world where life is growing and changing. The Jewel of the Creator is called Mother Earth.

Happiness and joy fills you and you raise your hands and say:

'Shining Star, Luc'ifer,

Thou art the torch-bearer,

Thou who brings light out of darkness,

Thou art the Shining One who greets us each dawning.

Your stellar light penetrates deep into the heart of the night.

Thou art the Lord of knowledge and desire,

Thou who shines with the light of truth

And illuminates all with your gentle radiance,

Without you Great Archangel Luc'ifer

We would truly be lost in Darkness.

Stand silently, and think about what you have uttered and what has been said to you. Ask yourself Pilgrim: Has this experience changed me? Think of what you have been privileged to see. Close your eyes and when you open them say these words:

'Eternal are the Archangels and Angels whose celestial realms endureth, forever and ever. I return thanks unto the Great Creator, in Whose Name thou, Luc'ifer hast come. Depart hence in peace unto thine habitations, and be thou ready to return when so ever I shall have called thee.'

Go through the portal into your world and seal the door behind you.

> 'May the Archangel Luc'ifer guard
> and bless you and keep you safe'

2
Archangel Mikh'ael
'Who is as God'

Legend

Titles that have been accredited to Archangel Mikh'ael include: Angel of Mercury, Leader of the Archangels, Prince of Virtues, Viceroy of Heaven, Angel of Earth, Guardian of Peace, Divine Protector, Angel of Sunday, Master of Balance, Angel of the Olive Tree, and Angel of the Almond Tree.

In Hebrew, *Mikh'ael* means 'who is like God' (*mi*-who. Ke-as or like El-deity) in Talmudic belief his name is interpreted as a rhetorical question: 'Who is like God?' which experts answer in the negative is to imply that *no one* is like God. Mikh'ael in this way is re-interpreted as a symbol of humility before God.

According to Judaic lore it was Mikh'ael who prevented Abraham 'from sacrificing his son Isaac.' Through legend it is told that he also appeared to Moses in the burning bush.

As the archangel of peace, harmony and balance, it is Mikh'ael who leads the angels of light (celestial army) in battle against the legions of angels of darkness. This phrase could be a metaphor for truth combating ignorance.

In the Dead Sea Scrolls there is reference to Wars of the Sons of Light where Mikh'ael is the Prince of Light battles against the Sons of Darkness led by the demon Belial. Some scholars interpret as 'Beli yo'il', from Hebrew translates as 'worthless'.

Much of the late Midrashic (study of biblical text) detail about Mikh'ael was conveyed to Christianity through the Book of Enoch and further elaborated on. Mikh'ael is designated in the Book of Enoch, as 'the prince of Israel' and the 'arci-strategy' of God. He is the angel of forbearance and mercy (*Enoch*, xl:3) who taught Enoch the mysteries of clemency and justice (lxxi:2).

Enoch 9:1 states that Mikh'ael, along with Rapha'el, Gabri'el, Uri'el and Suri'el heard the cries of men under the strain of the Watchers and their giant offspring. It was Mikh'ael and his compatriots who entreated God on behalf of men, prompting Yahweh to call Enoch to prophethood.

Some scholars consider Mikh'ael may be the angel in the book of Jubilees (i:27 and ii:1), who is said to have instructed Moses and delivered to him the tablets of Law on Mount Sinai.

In Greek folklore, St Mikh'ael also assumed the god Hermes role as the psychopomp escorting souls to Hades, and also in the role of weigher of souls on Judgment Day. According to a related folk belief, St Mikh'ael's face can only be seen by the dead and those about to die, and it is for this reason some folk icons portray him without a face.

Christian sects in the East first initiated Mikh'ael as a healer, and at the end of the fifth century in the West, as a patron of war. In late medieval Christianity, Mikh'ael, along with Saint George, became the patron saint of chivalry.

Jean Molinet, a fourteenth century French poet, chronicler and composer glorified the ancient feat of arms of the archangel as 'the first deed of knighthood and chivalrous prowess that was ever achieved.' Thus Mikh'ael was the natural patron of the first chivalric order of France; The Order of St Mikh'ael. In the British honours system, a chivalric order founded in 1818 is also named for these two saints, the Order of St Mikh'ael and St George. Mikh'ael is also considered in many Christian circles as the patron saint of the warrior. Police officers and soldiers, particularly paratroopers and fighter pilots regard Mikh'ael as their patron. The Catholic Police Guild has him as their patron. He is also a patron of Germany, City of Brussels and Kiev.

In the Middle Ages September 29 was celebrated as Mikh'ael's feast a day of obligation, as he was the patron of knights, but in the eighteenth century, along with several other feast days, it was gradually abolished. Mikh'aelmas Day, in England and other countries, was one of the regular quarter-days for settling rents and accounts; but it is no longer remarkable for the hospitality with which it was formerly celebrated. Traditionally, in the

British Isles, a well-fattened goose, fed on wheat stubble from the fields after harvest, is eaten to protect against financial need in the family for the next year, and as the saying goes:

> 'Eat a goose on Michaelmas Day,
> Want not for money all the year.'

In Scotland, St Michael's Bannock, or Struan Michi'el (a large stone-like cake) is baked. This used to be made from cereals moistened with sheep's milk, as sheep are regarded the most sacred of animals. The task of baking the bannock is given to the eldest daughter, and the following is said:

> 'Progeny and prosperity of family,
> Mystery of Michael, Protection of the Trinity'

Magical Intentions: Mikh'ael is the powerful protection angel and can be called upon to provide strength and courage. He helps with worldly ambitions, new jobs, in matters of acquiring money and favors from people in power. He aids work efforts involving business partnerships, work promotions, business ventures and professional success. In matters of health, ask his aid for any ailment of the spine or heart. He helps friendships, mental or physical health, bringing joy back into life are issues worked well on Sundays. Those who feel lost, he guides back on track as well as providing motivation. Working with the Archangel Mikh'ael will help remove fears, cut cords that attach you to another's energy and allow you to move freely along your divine path. His energy is powerful and engulfing. The light that we perceive is a part only of the infinite light, the few solar rays that correspond with our visual apparatus. The sun itself is a lamp adjusted to our dim sight; it is the luminous point in that space, which would be darkness to the eyes and our body, but like Mikh'ael, is resplendent for the intuition of our souls.

Rulerships: He governs all matters of ambition, personal success, anything to do with government affairs, and monarchy, such as kings and princes. All matters to do with creativity, music, composing and playing of instruments. He rules everything made of gold, and is present on Golden Wedding

Anniversaries. Mikh'ael especially, rules wedding rings, as it represents a golden circle made by the Sun disk. Bridal orange blossom is sacred to him, and he is certainly present at all weddings. He oversees personal fulfilment, power, pride, and promotion. He applauds self-confidence and is by your side through your success.

Negative aspects: Arrogance, bigotry and pride.

As Archangel Mikh'ael is a Higher Angel, he rules only one sign – the sun, which he uses to transmit messages via sunbeams. Most other angels rule two signs, Archangel Mikh'ael, Gabri'el and Uri'el being the exception.

He is the Archangel for those born under the sign of Leo ♌. He is of the four winds and his orientation is south. Being 'warrior-like', his energy colour is red, element fire and his season is summer. Mikh'ael's main symbol is that of the sword, sometimes represented as a flame bursting forth from the hilt. Colours representative of Mikh'ael are: gold, yellow, and rose.

Throughout the pathworking many signs and symbolic forms will be revealed to you and it is important that you remember them, especially if you intend writing letters of petition.

When writing to Archangel Mikh'ael, first draw his three symbols, write: 'To the Archangel Mikh'ael' in Passing the River Script, the request in Theban Script, and finally sign your secret name in Passing the Rivers Script.

Letters to Archangel Mikh'ael must be written on a Sunday at his appointed hour. (see chart) using yellow paper and purple ink.

When you have written your letter to him, keep it for seven days - from Sunday to Sunday. During this time, you will in most cases, receive a sign that your request is to be granted. Burn the letter the following Sunday. Should you not receive any sign, <u>do not</u> repeat your letters until a month has passed i.e. four Sundays have elapsed. Signs will not be given to you until the time is right.

Magical letters can be written to any of the Ruling Angels but only on matters they rule, and on their day, on matters you need to invoke or banish.

Do not complicate this system beyond what is given, as the letter is sufficient. Simplicity is the beauty of this art, the Voice of Angels is not a ritual, add the knowledge to what you already have and don't confuse systems.

> 'May the Archangel Mikh'ael grant
> and bless your request'

Path to Archangel Mikh'ael

What you will need:
Oil of frankincense, incense, charcoal, goblet of wine/beer, fruit juice or water, two orange candles, a statue or picture of the angel (optional but very useful).

Preparation:
Don your white robe and tie a red cord around your waist. This will be in respect for the Angel you will be working with. Anoint wrists, temples and throat with oil of frankincense. Light candles. Prepare charcoal and add incense as required. Fill goblet with liquid and raise it in salutation to the angels and place it back on your altar.

Sit comfortably in an upright chair and inhale very slowly and deeply. You are not just inhaling air, but joy, serenity, strength, vitality, courage, and whichever positive quality you want to affirm. Imagine the breath filling not only your lungs, but also the whole body – starting from the feet and culminating at a point between the eyebrows.

As you exhale not only do you expel carbon dioxide from your system, but also mental and emotional impurities such as weakness, discouragement and despair. Feel the intimate connection between the mind and the breath. Feel the flow of energy around your body as you prepare for your ritual working.

Say the temple prayer to the angels:

I call upon thy sacred name

Of the being that has been with me

Since the beginning of beginnings.

As I gaze upwards,

May I behold thy beauty and thy splendour unto eternity,

Time without end.

Build your gate with love and care; visualise Angel Hair quartz crystal the colour of citrine pushing up through the earth, towering above your head and disappearing into the heavens. Visualise a brilliant shaft of light pass through it. Marvel at the smoky golden brown strands tipped with red sparks of colour as spirits dance within. Feel the warmth of sunbeams as you pass through the gleaming portal. Inner voices ring out: 'All man is Divine' – feel the words within your heart.

You are unnerved; as again you stand on a ten-edged crystal platform that floats above the yawning abyss, and are gladdened when Luc'ifer suddenly appears before you and smiling broadly. He takes you by your left hand, and together you walk clockwise round the perimeter of the platform, and traces a line through the air with his left hand. The atmosphere splits as ten crystal walls erupt from the abyss and tower above.

Inside each milky opalescent cell a divine image gazes curiously out. Luc'ifer points to cell and tells you to touch the surface that is warm against your fingers. Fabulous colours beyond the spectrum dazzle you – colours that are in complete harmony with a multitude of voices that saturate the crystal walls. The sound turns to a ringing in your ears causing you to cup your hands against each side of your head. Within the cacophony you hear a word – or is it a name? Luc'ifer senses your discomfort and holds up his hand, the voices fall silent, misty divine images gaze curiously through the crystal – beyond, untold mysteries await you.

It is time to call forth the archangel.

Pause before beginning your invocation. Visualise each word as you utter it. Breathe it into life; endow it with passion and sincerity. Each is a rhythmic element combining to form a powerful symphony, imbue your call with such beauty that the angelic being cannot but help to respond. Not only will you be invoking Mikh'ael, but going on a journey into the centre of his realm. You will learn how to focus on his energy as you are drawn in. This is your gateway. Say:

'O Great Warrior Spirit,

Leader of the Archangels,

Receive me into your realm.

Open my heart and my mind

That I may feel you and know you.

Thou who is Master of all Angels,

I pray thee, show me a sign.'

Emblazoned on one of the cell walls is the signature of the Archangel Mikh'ael.

Mikh'ael

Mikh -A-EL

Commit it to memory. This symbol is charged, look at each mark and take it within. A rivulet of fire forms around your feet, the tiny flames turn into salamanders that lick your ankles – but instead of burning you; their tender tongues are warm and caress your skin like gentle kisses. The crystal wall melts away.

Pungent smelling red gaseous clouds suddenly lift and float you and your guardian Luc'ifer on high to an entrance flagged on either side by two monolithic columns of flame; each pulsates with energy that ascend into your spirit. Luc'ifer strides forward and gestures for you to follow him.

You walk between the towering columns of fire; your body bathed in the power of the sun and above you is a sky of electric blue. Happiness and joy fills you and you raise your hands and say:

'Come, Heavenly Spirits adorned in the radiance of the Sun

Luminous Spirits who are ready to obey the power of the Tetragrammaton.

Come, assist me in the operation that I am making with the help of the

Grand light of Day, which the Eternal Creator hath formed for the use of

Universal nature.

I invoke thee for these purposes.

I pray thee, be favourable to what I shall ask

In the Name of Amioram, Adonai, Sabaoth.'

Pause to allow your conscious mind to take in events so far, let it become like a clear pool, allowing light through and reflecting the stillness of the skies above.

Beneath your feet spring a carpet of bright marigolds and orchids; beautiful flowers typify the rising Sun, and the divine gift of eternal youth. Butterflies alight, their wings as golden as the Sun itself. You do not fear the daddy-long legs spiders that crawl across your toes. Unexpectedly a field of sunflowers burst forth turning their orange-yellow heads towards a giant sun. The air is made fragrant as a sweet-scented breeze rustles the branches of laurel trees. But within the breeze is a word – a sound – a name.

Meditate:

Pilgrim, contemplate why you are on this path. Think about what your name should be. Often nature will leave clues along the way. Re-learn the magic of your name and the mystery of its sound, let it vibrate and sing within you, and say:

Let my name be known as……….
(Choose your secret magical name)

Lo, my name shall be my password.

May it bridge earth, sky and heaven.

I solemnly vow to guard it with care.

It is the sum of all I have been, what I am and will be.

May it be Power, Divinity and Wisdom encapsulated!

I fear not the mystery of heat,

In the mystery of silence that softly showers out of the Sun.'

Feel the energy rise as wave after wave of sound travels to the furthest reaches of the Universe and back again. It will reach its destination in good time, be patient and receptive.

The Conjuration

'O ye Spirits, ye I conjure

By the Power, Wisdom,
and Virtue of the Spirit of the Great One,

By the uncreate Divine Knowledge,

By the vast Mercy of the Creator,

By the Strength of the Creator,

By the Greatness of the Creator,

By the Unity of the Creator,

Ruler of the Seventh Heaven Machen

And by the planet name of Shem-esh!

May the Archangel Mikh'ael,

Appear before me!'

The air is saturated with the heady scent of cinnamon mingled with myrrh and amber; this serves to heighten your awareness, Pilgrim. Your lungs are heavy with each intake of breath. Say:

'In wild delight I see fiery creatures rush from all sides,

In great conflagration they fly upwards surrounding a high golden throne

Red flames engulf a Great Being

Hail Great One! Hail Mikh'ael!

You appear before me and I tremble at your presence.

Thou who wears the robes of scarlet

Thou who carries the flaming sword
Thou who holds the shield of gold
I perceive a talisman of strange design

The light of which hurts my eyes.
I behold a wondrous being
Golden as the clouds of heaven
Golden is your hallowed head
Golden is your crown
Radiant is your wondrous face
I stand before you spellbound as your bright eyes pierce my very soul.'

The Archangel Mikh'ael's gaze is steady, but it is not on you – it is on Luc'ifer. The air around you is electric. Aqui'el, the ethereal soul of the Moon hovers above Mikh'ael's head, ever alert waiting for a command from his master. To the left stands the angel Sorath, emblazoned on his chest is the planetary symbol of the spirit of the Sun. To the right of Mikh'ael is the angel Nakhi'el, on his forehead is the imprint of symbol of intelligence. Aqui'el slowly flaps his wings above your head causing your robe to gently move about you. His black steely eyes penetrate your very being. The very nearness of him turns your stomach – he has the stench of a thousand rotting corpses.

Mikh'ael steps down from his throne pointing his fiery sword at Luc'ifer who stands defiant observing the expression on his brother's face – Mikh'ael is not at ease.

'Yls chis loncho madriax, O Githgulcag, Nor de Iaod Basgim. Brints unig canse gah.'

'How thou art fallen from heaven, O Luc'ifer, Son of the Morning,

It has taken a brave soul to release you.'

Sorath and Nachi'el become agitated, their talismans vibrate with the charge of electricity around them. Luc'ifer smiles broadly, dismissing Mikh'ael's comment, and answers:

'Ol Fetharzi!'

I visit in peace!'

Luc'ifer's voice is surly. You sense the tension between the two angels but can do nothing but observe. Mikh'ael holds his sword more as a protective measure than an emblem. The flames flicker and splutter against his bright golden shield, the incised talisman glints sending out a myriad of light.

Luc'ifer absorbs the light with a mere sniff to the air plunging Mikh'ael into shadow, and says:

'Zorge, Mikha'el! Lap zirdo noco mad.

Hoath Iaida.'

'Be friendly unto me Mikh'ael!

For I am the servant of the same God

The true worshiper of the Highest.'

Luc'ifer plucks from the air a golden platter laden with oranges and pomegranates and indicates that you offer it to Mikh'ael. The archangel smiles and nods his head and returns to the high podium. Behind Mikh'ael's throne prowls a lion – without taking his eyes off you, Mikh'ael lays down his fiery sword and gently caresses the course fur of the mighty king of beasts.

On an altar in front of you are laurel leaves, cinnamon, aloes wood, musk, cloves, myrrh and a crucible of burning charcoals. These represent the incense of the Sun. Take a handful and cast them into the glowing charcoals and say:

'I pray thee Archangel Mikh'ael

Protector and gracious angel of the flame,

Receive these perfumed fumigations.

May the rising flames from these herbs

Ignite my courage and send it into your realm.

I bow to thee Mikh'ael,

Thou who sits ever-waiting and ever-present,

Thou who forever guards the threshold of divine truths,

I open my heart to you

And rejoice in your presence.'

From the ether a black cat leaps onto the altar, its large green eyes survey you whilst pawing the double-sided Kamea that has appeared on the sacred Table of the Sun.

6	32	3	34	35	1
7	11	27	28	8	30
24	14	16	15	23	19
13	20	22	21	17	18
25	29	10	9	26	12
36	5	33	4	2	31

It is written on a sliver of yellow metal so fine it wafts upwards, only to be snatched away by Luc'ifer who crumbles it to gold dust sprinkling it over your head. As it falls a voice utters:

'Within this square are divine names, Pilgrim, of the Intelligence and Spirit – sacred to Mikh'ael through the Sun.'

In silence you look up at the archangel. His face shimmers, but not with the light of the Sun, but that of an alien being. The once glorious orbs of eyes now resemble those of a serpent – these eyes now absorb you. Enter the body of the archangel, and merge with his being. Look through the archangel's eyes upon yourself. Take in what you see Pilgrim.

A mass of energy forms behind you – no face is visible but you know it is the Great Creator. Turmoil is erupting within the central core of his being, and a story begins to unfold.

Luc'ifer is in paradise; he is a high and exalted angel who sits at the right hand of the Creator. Luc'ifer's countenance is gentle and expresses such joy and happiness it ripples out and touches all around him. With intelligence, radiance, beauty, and a power unmatched among all of his angelic brethren, He is second in majesty only to the Creator Himself. You feel a shudder go through the Archangel Mikh'ael as he whispers:

'His form is perfect, his bearing noble and majestic. Wondrous is the light that beams in my brother Luc'ifer's face. How it shines around him brighter and more beautiful than around any of the other angels.'

You can do nothing as look on through the gaze of Mikh'ael feeling his anguish. Statue-like, your form remains rooted to the spot whilst the turmoil within the heavens continues. The Son of the Morning speaks:

'It was *I*, Luc'ifer, who was favourite in the heavens among the angels. It was *I* who was chosen to be near the great Creator, and the ceaseless beams of glorious light enshrouding the eternal One at the beginning of time. The first light ever, also shone upon me. Once, all angels obeyed my command with pleasurable alacrity. I had a special mission to execute until *you*, Mikh'ael and that other brother Gabri'el interfered!'

Mikh'ael is envious of his brother and screams:

'True, my brother Luc'ifer, you were highly exalted, but you did not call forth gratitude and praise to our Divine Creator. You aspired to the height of the Creator Himself! You glorified in your loftiness. Your special mission was to take over our celestial realm. It is *I*, Mikh'ael who bears the title 'Who is as God!"

With that last outburst you are back in your body looking up at the Archangel Mikh'ael. Light radiates in great waves from his body, impacting on your senses. Luc'ifer stands beside you and bows his head to his brother.

It is at this stage where you may want to take some personal time with Mikh'ael for quiet introspection, conversation, meditation or whatever you need to build and cultivate your relationship with the archangel. Say:

'Great Archangel Mikh'ael I pray thee,

Open my eyes so that I may see the sacred.'

Mikh'ael nods his head to his brother Luc'ifer who stands in front of you holding a ring of pure gold. Attached to the band, a square plate with the letters 'PELE' inscribed in the four corners, Hebrew for 'Workers of wonders'. In the centre, a circle with a horizontal line going through it, with the letter 'V' above and the letter 'L' below.

'Pilgrim this is the sacred ring worn by Solomon.'

As you put the ring on the index finger of your right hand, Luc'ifer places a crimson red silk tabard over your head; the weight is heavy on your shoulders. Embroidered on the front in golden threads is the lamen designed to control negative forces.

Look at the letters Pilgrim 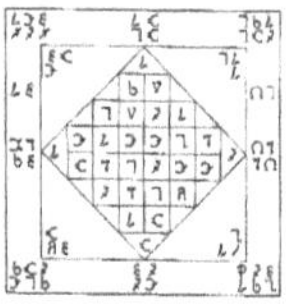 take in the energy, feel the power of the ring and say:

'Show me the link between the divine and earthly powers.'

The air is stilled - silence is all around you. The archangel Mikh'ael looks on. A crystal table materializes before you, and in the centre is incised the six-pointed Shield of David.

The buzzing of a thousand bees fills the air breaking the silence. The great swarm covers the beautiful table with liquid wax. The bees disperse leaving behind them a complex circle of interlacing stars and heptagons. You strain your eyes on the fabulous design, but suddenly the centre blurs from your vision leaving just the outer ring. Mikh'ael's powerful voice is carried above the cacophony as he utters:

'Aleph-Mem-Tav!

Pilgrim, in time,

This will be opened unto thee

This is holy

This is pure

This is forever!

But thou mayest marvel only the outer ring.

It is your first step,

And when thou art ready Pilgrim,

More will be revealed.

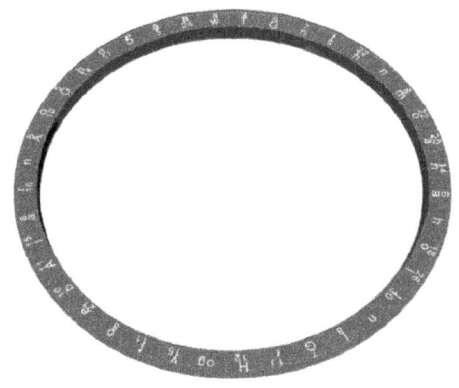

The ring spins upward, hovers above your head, and gently settles on the ground in front of you. Wave upon wave of letters, numbers and symbols impact upon you, but what do they mean?

In a dream-state you say:

'Ye I Behold the Greatest Name of God.

O that I may touch the hallowed name

So that I may be at one with the Great Creator.'

You walk forward onto the edge of the ring, in its centre is a fathomless void; a mystery force of dark energy slowly begins to drag you in. You pull yourself back falling onto the rim of the circle. The warmth of your fingers melts the wax of the ring and a dense mist forms like a heavy curtain obliterating all before you.

A hand gently touches you on the shoulder causing you to look up, it is Luc'ifer who smiles and indicates that it is time for you to leave the angelic realm of Mikh'ael.

Stand silently, and think about what you have uttered and what has been said to you. Ask yourself Pilgrim: Has this experience changed me?

Think of what you have been privileged to see. Close your eyes and when you open them say these words:

'Eternal are the Archangels and Angels whose celestial realms endureth, forever and ever. I return thanks unto the Great Creator, in Whose Name thou, Mikh'ael hast come. Depart hence in peace unto thine habitations, and be thou ready to return when so ever I shall have called thee.'

Utter your secret name to the angels, go through the portal into your world and seal the door behind you.

3
Archangel Gabri'el
'God is my strength'

Legend

Countless titles have been given to Gabri'el through many different sources; Ruler of the South Heaven, Chief Ambassador to Humanity, Chief Ambassador to God, Divine Herald, Prince of Justice, Angel of Aspirations, Angel of Truth, Angel of Revelation, Divine Husband, Angel of Joy, Angel of Childbirth, Archangel of the Holy Sefirot, Trumpeter of the Last Judgment, Ruling Prince of the Cherubim, Angel of Vengeance, Angel of Death, Angel of Mercy, Angel of Judgment, Governor of Eden, and Angel of the Apple Tree.

Gabri'el comes from the Hebrew meaning 'Man of God.' It has alternately been translated 'God is mighty' or 'the strength/power of God.' The Prologue from Orphid explains his name this way: 'Man-God'. Gabri'el has also been interpreted to mean 'God is my strength.'

His origins are Chaldean, and it is believed that he was worshipped as a Babylonian goddess who was later transformed into an archangel (as were both Archangels Mikh'ael and Rapha'el). It is said that Gabri'el sits at the left hand side of God, the left being feminine. In the Seventh Heaven he is the ruler of the cherubim (the order of angels who act as intermediaries carrying out God's will).

Apart from Mikh'ael, he is the only angel mentioned by name in the Old Testament - unless we include among the *Book of Tobit* in the Apocrypha, in which case Rapha'el, who appears there, becomes the third named angel. Only four appearances of Gabri'el are recorded: In Dani'el 8, he explains the vision of the horned ram as foretelling the destruction of the Persian Empire by the Macedonian Alexander the Great, after whose death the kingdom will be divided up among his generals, from one of whom will spring Antiochus Epiphanes. In chapter 9, after Dani'el had prayed for Israel, we read that 'the man Gabri'el . . .. flying swiftly touched me' and he communicated to him the mysterious prophecy of the 'seventy weeks' of years that should elapse before the coming of the Messiah or Liberator.

Though seemingly feminine in nature, Gabri'el is also an angel of great power. It is believed that it is Gabri'el who brought down the cities of Sodom and Gomorrah, he was also instrumental in parting the waters of the Read Sea when Moses led his people to safety away from the Egyptian armies, and it was also He who inspired Joan of Arc to help the Dauphin.

Gabri'el is called the bringer of good news for throughout much of the scriptures and ancient texts he has been known to bring tidings of joy and happiness. He also helps those with talents in art and communication. During the middle ages, Christians believed him to be the angel of light.

Known as the angel of annunciation, it was Gabri'el who brought the news to Mary that she would give birth to a child. He also announced to Zechariah that his wife, Elizabeth, would give birth to John the Baptist (Elizabeth was Mary's cousin). It is said that Gabri'el struck Zechariah mute for not believing her!

The Jews venerated Gabri'el as the angel of judgment, and in both Jewish and Christian tradition he is one of the seven archangels. Gabri'el is also known to Moslems, as Jibril and they believe him to be the angel who served as the mouthpiece of the Great Creator in dictating the Koran to Mohammed and presented the Black Stone of the Kaba to Abraham in Mecca. To this day thousands of people travel to Mecca to kiss this stone.

Christian tradition sites Gabri'el as the trumpeter of the Last Judgment (1 Thes. 4.16). In art and literature Gabri'el is mainly treated as the Angel of the Annunciation and is portrayed carrying a lily, the symbol of the Virgin. He is often represented on churches with trumpet raised and facing east, ready to proclaim the second coming of Christ.

Gabri'el is Archangel of the Moon, and according to the moon's phases he is empowered to aid you. By understanding the moon tides can save you unnecessary effort when you do magic. These phases control, amongst other things, the ebb and flow of the etheric force that is essential to successful ritual magic.

Rulership: Archangel Gabri'el is known as the archangel of revelation, creativity, and faith and bestows upon you imagination and clairvoyance. He controls the ebb and flow of fortune, increase in all things physical and domestic affairs of women, and matters of the home. He rules conception and is also the angel of childbirth who guides the unborn souls until they enter this world. It is said that the cleft just above the lip is where Gabri'el touches the unborn soul and tells them: 'shhh….do not share any of the secrets of Heaven'. He is the patron saint of midwives, nurses, doctors, and all those who provide care throughout pregnancy and childbirth, teachers, nannies, messengers and all forms of communication and media. Gabri'el guards you on a long journey and travel by sea.

You may petition on the following:

Health matters of all kinds to do with feminine functions of the body and reproductive organs; ailments of the breast (in women) ailments caused by childbirth for sterility in women, for water retention in both sexes, and to cure warts in both sexes; all matters of home and domestic equipment. For help and safeguard during journeys by land and sea, also guard against seasickness. He helps make fertile and increase anything at all (except love affairs and money), he looks after women generally, and aids the curing of stomach complaints.

He is the Archangel for those who were born under the sign of Cancer ♋. Gabri'el is of the four winds, and his orientation is west. Being 'nature-like', his energy colour is green and blue-green. His element is Water, and His season is winter.

Gabri'el's symbol is that of a trumpet. Colours representative of him are silver and white.

Throughout the pathworking many signs and symbolic forms will be revealed to you and it is important that you remember them, especially if you intend writing letters of petition.

When writing to this angel, first draw his three symbols, write 'To Archangel Gabri'el' followed by the letter of request, all of which is written in Theban Script and finally sign your secret name in Passing the Rivers Script.

It may be written on a Monday appointed hour (see chart), a new moon, or a full moon using white paper and blue ink. The letter is kept for a lunar cycle, or twenty-eight days. The day of writing counts as one day, and on the twenty-eighth day, the letter is burnt.

Gabri'el may use one or several of the signs during the course of the twenty-eight days, but one sign is enough to assume your request has been granted.

If you receive no sign from Gabri'el, your request is refused. Magical help is not intended to take the place of your own efforts.

Magical letters can be written to any of the Ruling Angels but only on matters He rules, and on His day, you need to invoke or banish. Do not complicate this system beyond what is given, as the letter is sufficient. Simplicity is the beauty of this art, the Voice of Angels is not a ritual, add the knowledge to what you already have and don't confuse systems.

> 'May the Archangel Gabri'el grant
> and bless your request'

Path To Gabri'el

What you will need:
Oil of frankincense, incense, charcoal, goblet of wine/beer, fruit juice or water, two white candles, a statue or picture of the angel (optional but very useful).

Preparation:
Don your white robe and tie a silver and blue cord around your waist. This will be in respect for the Angel you will be working with. Anoint wrists, temples and throat with oil of frankincense. Light candles. Prepare charcoal and add incense as required. Fill goblet with liquid and raise it in salutation to the angels and place it back on your altar.

Sit comfortably in an upright chair and inhale very slowly and deeply. You are not just inhaling air, but joy, serenity, strength, vitality, courage, and whichever positive quality you want to affirm. Imagine the breath filling not only your lungs, but also the whole body – starting from the feet and culminating at a point between the eyebrows.

As you exhale not only do you expel carbon dioxide from your system, but also mental and emotional impurities such as weakness, discouragement and despair. Feel the intimate connection between the mind and the breath. Feel the flow of energy around your body as you prepare for your ritual working.

Say the temple prayer to the angels:

I call upon thy sacred name

Of the being that has been with me

Since the beginning of beginnings.

As I gaze upwards

May I behold thy beauty and thy splendour unto eternity,

Time without end.

Build your gate with love and care; visualise Angel Hair quartz crystal the colour of citrine pushing up through the earth, towering above your head and disappearing into the heavens. Visualise a brilliant shaft of light pass through it. Marvel at the smoky golden brown strands tipped with red sparks of colour as spirits dance within. Feel the cool of moonbeams as you pass through the gleaming portal.

Cross over to the beyond Pilgrim, don't be afraid. Hovering above the abyss the ten-edged crystal platform glints in an opalescent glow, and through this lovely light your guardian Luc'ifer walks. His beautiful face radiates – welcome – and all your fears are banished.

Without taking his eyes off you, he waves his right hand in the air in a clockwise motion bringing forth ten crystal cells. Inner voices ring out: 'All man is Divine' – feel the words within your heart.

A strange moon dust levitates about you, these tiny particles constantly leap up and down off the surface of the moon – yes Pilgrim and you are on the lunar surface, in the realm of Gabri'el. The sky appears dark, even on the bright side of the moon, due to the lack of atmosphere. It is a silent place, making it difficult to transmit sound. Through the low lunar altitude, projects a fine point of light. Through this thin veil call forth the Archangel Gabri'el.

Before beginning your invocation, visualise each word as you utter it. Breathe it into life; endow it with passion and sincerity. Each is a rhythmic element combining to form a powerful symphony, imbue your call with such beauty that the angelic being cannot but help to respond. Not only will you be invoking Gabri'el, but going on a journey into the centre of his realm. You will learn how to focus on his energy as you are drawn in. This is your gateway.

Great Messenger!

Defender of the element of water,

Angel of Resurrection,

Divine protector of children,

Receive me into your realm.

Open my heart and my mind

That I may feel you and know you.

Thou who art Ruler of the First Heaven

Watcher of the South,

I pray thee, show me a sign.'

Like cold fire the signature of the Archangel Gabri'el is emblazoned on one of the cell walls.

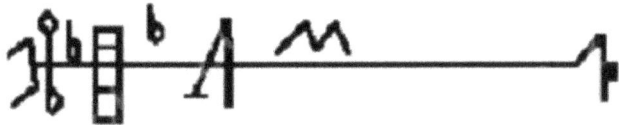

Gabri'el

gay- BREE-EL.

Commit it to memory. This symbol is charged, look at each mark and take it within. A pool of liquid moonshine in the shape of a crescent forms at your feet. As you step into it gentle ripples create chords of music so beautiful you close your eyes drinking in the sounds. Like a cascade, the wall of crystal liquefies poring forth every phase of the moon. Luc'ifer steps forward scooping up a full moon. As he places it in your hands it turns into a glassy orb. Pilgrim, this is no ordinary orb, as within it, are all the signs and symbols of Gabri'el. Look into it and say:

'Come, Spirits adorned in the luminosity of the Moon,

Radiant Spirits who are ready to obey the power of the ancient tongue,

Come, assist me in the operation that I am making with the aid of the

Majestic light of the Moon the Eternal Creator hath formed.

I invoke thee for these purposes.

I pray thee, be favourable to what I shall ask.

In the Name of the beings who surround and reflect the Mighty Gabri'el,

Heavenly angel, guard me.'

You are standing beneath a Willow tree that gently sways; its long frothy branches caress grasses be-speckled with tiny white flowers; their fragile forms almost too delicate to walk upon. Moths alight and spiders weave their gossamer fine webs amongst the leaves. A wondrous fragrance is all about you, hanging heavy in the air. Say:

'Hail Gabri'el

I pray thee, with each intake of breath

May the aroma serve to intensify my awareness of thee.'

Pause to allow your conscious mind to take in events so far, let it become like a clear pool, allowing light through and reflecting the stillness of the skies above.

Conjuration

I ….. (utter your secret name) salute thee and conjure thee,

O beautiful Moon,

O most beautiful Planet,

O light of which I have in my hand.

By the air that I breathe within me,

By the orb I am touching: I conjure thee.

By the names of the spirit princes living in you,

By the ineffable name on which created everything!

By you, O resplendent One, appear!

And by the planet name of LBNH

Ruler of the First Heaven Shamain

Grace my eyes with your presence

Archangel Gabri'el, appear before me!

ANGELIC MAGICK

The orb in your hands vaporises into a bright light followed by a blast of trumpets. A heady fragrance of lilies pervades the air. Drink in the aroma Pilgrim, and say:

Bless-ed be He,

Bless-ed be the Archangel

Bless-ed be He

Hail Great One! Hail Gabri'el!

Thou who now stands before me

Thou whose face is framed by long silver hair

A silver crescent moon adorns your proud brow,

Shining is your wondrous face

Powerful is your form clad in raiment of silver and white.

Delicate is the lily cradled in your mighty left arm

Glorious are the moonbeams that surround your Being.

From within the light I perceive a talisman of strange design

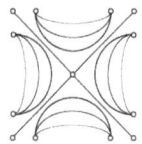

I pray that I shall know it's meaning.

I, a mere mortal stand before you awestruck

Your gaze and piercing eyes capture my soul.

The light of which hurts my eyes.

May that the light I perceive not blind me.

May that the aroma I inhale not choke me.'

Drifting through the haze of moonbeams is a creature so fantastic you grip the arm of Luc'ifer. Ashmodai; the planetary spirit its ethereal soul of the moon hovers above Gabri'el's head;

his sigil pulsates across his chest 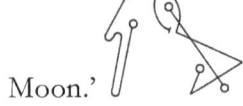. Ashmodai's presence doesn't distract from Gabri'el's gaze, but it is not on you. He is looking at Luc'ifer who bows low to his younger brother.

'Yls chis parach, esiasch, torzu od biab. Moz comselh. Gchisge yls Pir de Basgim?'

'You are equal in all ways my brother, rise and stand with me. My love is all around you. Are you not my Daemon of the Day?'

The two brothers embrace, their emotions send waves throughout he universe and beyond.

In quick succession other creatures appear. Their thin voices vibrate their sigils illuminating their shining forms.

'I am Shad Barschemoth Ha-Schartathan, Spirit of Spirits of the Moon.'

'I am Malkah he Tarshisim Ve-ad Ruachoth Ha- Schekalim, Intelligence of the Intelligencies of the Moon.'

They chime in unison:

'We are the presiding angels that are set over the planets.'

In a grand gesture Archangel Gabri'el waves the fragile lily as a wand materialising a banqueting table brimming with fine foods. Silver platters of crab and shellfish of all kinds; succulent melons sliced in wedges, the juices glisten in the moonlight, milky-white lychees oozing syrup onto plump pale yellow pears. Centred in the middle of the table is a crystal dish holding Camphor, Jasmine, Frankincense, White Sandalwood and a silver crucible of burning coals.

From under the table crawls a dog lifting his head to bay at the moon. A seagull flies above and a lone owl hoots from within the branches of the weeping willow. A white peacock struts elegantly towards you and in its beak, is a sliver of silver, the Kamea. Take it Pilgrim and look at both sides it is the numbers sacred only to the moon.

37	78	29	70	21	62	13	54	5
6	38	79	30	71	22	63	14	46
47	7	39	80	31	72	23	55	15
16	48	8	40	81	32	64	24	56
57	17	49	9	41	73	33	65	25
26	58	18	50	1	42	74	34	66
67	27	59	10	51	2	43	75	35
36	68	19	60	11	52	3	44	76
77	28	69	20	61	12	53	4	45

What do they mean? You hear yourself say. The silver dissolves into the palm of your hand and as it does, the sacred numbers impact on your inner psyche. You hear a voice say:

'Within this square are divine names, Pilgrim, the names of the Intelligence and spirit of spirits sacred to Gabri'el through the Moon.'

Walk forward and take a handful of incense and cast it onto the burning coals and say:

'I pray thee Archangel Gabri'el

Protector and gracious angel of the Moon,

Receive these perfumed fumigations

May the rising flames from these herbs

Ignite my courage and send it into your realm.

I bow to thee Gabri'el who sits ever-waiting and ever-present,

Thou who forever guards the threshold of divine truths,

I open my heart to you

And rejoice in your presence.'

Gabri'el whispers into his brother Luc'ifer's ear, and from a pocket in his robe Luc'ifer retrieves the sacred ring of Solomon. Take the ring Pilgrim and put it on the index finger of your right hand:

An angelic being drifts forward and passes a crimson red silk tabard to Luc'ifer who takes it and places it over your shoulders. Feel the power and energy. Listen to voice of Gabri'el.

'Ror I ta nazpsad, graa ta malpurg:
Casarm holq qaa nothoa zimz.'

'The Sun is as a sword, and the Moon as a through-thrusting fire: Who measureth your garments in the midst of my vestures'

It is at this stage where you may want to take some personal time with Gabri'el for quiet introspection, conversation, meditation or whatever you need to build and cultivate your relationship with the archangel. Say:

Great Archangel Gabri'el I pray thee,

'Odo cicle qaa. Odo ooaona arpuran Pirgah.'

'Open my eyes so that I may see the sacred.'

Archangel Gabri'el smiles and with his right hand creates a great wax disc that spins slowly in the air in front of you, and utters:

'Aleph-Mem-Tav.'

ANGELIC MAGICK

'Pilgrim, take in all you see, reflect on the mystery within.'

The wax disc settles in front of you and stills, revealing more complex rings and concentric circles, but the centre is a swirling mass of chaos. Gabri'el continues:

'Pilgrim, I give you a riddle. Seven of the letters are in capitals signifying the first of certain angelic names. To find these names use the numbers connected with each letter. When the number is above the letter, count that many letters clockwise to find the next letter of the name; when the number is below the letter, count, counter clockwise. Each name will end when you reach one of the six letters without a number.'

This is indeed a test Pilgrim. Look carefully and take in the essence. Moments pass, Luc'ifer and Gabri'el look on. The rims become transparent and pale into the ether revealing just a ghost of the original form. You want to look down but are unable too. Vibrating through the soles of your feet to your heart the letters whisper:

'These are the seven 'Names of the Great Creator, not known to the Angels; neither can be spoken nor read by man. The true name of the Great Creator is known neither to men nor to Angels, but to the Holy One alone.'

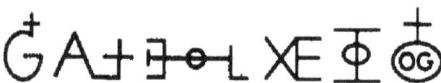

'Ga-le-thog '

Take a deep breath and say:

'Great Archangel of the Moon,

Thou art most splendid in thy magic,

I am honoured to behold the mystery within.

O that I may thank thee!'

From beyond the veil another voice reaches you, one that you have not heard before; a dense grey cloud covers his giant form, it is Archangel Uri'el, his words travel along a lightning flash:

'Pilgrim! Of these seven names every letter contains an Angel of Brightness known only to the Great Creator Himself. A sufficient bond to compel all creatures to life or death, or anything else contained on the earth.'

Gabri'el has disappeared from view and only Luc'ifer is beside you. For a brief moment a great seal appears and you strain your eyes to take in the centre of the disc but it dissolves into the ether taking the outer rims with it.

Darkness closes around you causing you to shiver, be not afraid Pilgrim, for it is now time for you to leave the angelic realm of Gabri'el.

Stand silently, and think about what you have uttered, what has been said to you and foremost, what has been revealed. Ask yourself Pilgrim: Has this experience changed me?

Close your eyes and when you open them say these words:

'Eternal are the Archangels and Angels whose celestial realms endureth, forever and ever. I return thanks unto the Great Creator, in Whose Name thou, Gabri'el hast come. Depart hence in peace unto thine habitations, and be thou ready to return when so ever I shall have need of thee.'

Utter your secret name to the angels, go through the portal into your world and seal the door behind you.

'May the Archangel Gabri'el guard
and bless you and keep you safe'

4
Archangel Sama'el
'Venom of God'

Legend

The etymology of his name is a combination of 'sam' meaning 'poison' or 'venom', and 'el', meaning God'; hence he is Venom/Poison of God. Other names he is known by are Sammael and Samil. In legend this archangel is considered both a member of the heavenly host and like Luc'ifer, a fallen angel to be compared with Satan and chief of evil spirits.

One of Sama'el's greatest roles in Jewish lore is angel of death and destruction and is often incorrectly equated in the Book of Revelation as Apollyon. In this capacity he is a fallen angel but nevertheless remains one of God's servants.

As a good angel, Sama'el supposedly resides in the seventh heaven, although he is declared to be the chief angel of the fifth heaven and Prince of the Seraphim.

Sama'el is an important archangel in the Talmudic and post-Talmudic lore, a figure that is accuser, seducer and destroyer. In rabbinic lore he is identified as 'Satan Kanom'.

In the Secrets of Enoch (Enoch II) he is a magician and prince of demons. Sama'el was also patron of the Empire of Rome.

Yalkut 1, 110 of the Talmud speaks of Sama'el as Esau's guardian angel, and in the Sayings of Rabbi Eliezer, he is charged with being the one who tempted Eve, then seduced and impregnated her with Cain. Although some sources identify Gadre-el as the angel and seducer of Eve, other Hebrew scholars say it was Sama'el in the guise of the serpent.

Sama'el is sometimes identified as being the angelic antagonist who wrestled with Jacob, and also the angel who held back the arm of Abraham as he was about to sacrifice his son Isaac.

According to *The Ascension of Moses* (Chapter IV - Aggadah - The Legend of The Jews - by Louis Ginzberg) Sama'el is also mentioned as being in 7th Heaven:

> 'In the last heaven Moses saw two angels, each five hundred parasangs in height, forged out of chains of black fire and red fire, the angels Af, "Anger," and Hemah, "Wrath," whom God created at the beginning of the world, to execute His will. Moses was disquieted when he looked upon them, but Metatron embraced him, and said, "Moses, Moses, thou favourite of God, fear not, and be not terrified," and Moses became calm. There was another angel in the seventh heaven, different in appearance from all the others, and of frightful mien. His height was so great, it would have taken five hundred years to cover a distance equal to it, and from the crown of his head to the soles of his feet he was studded with glaring eyes, at the sight of which the beholder fell prostrate in awe. "This one," said Metatron, addressing Moses, "is Sama'el, who takes the soul away from man." "Whither goes he now?" asked Moses, and Metatron replied, "To fetch the soul of Job the pious." Thereupon Moses prayed to God in these words, "O may it be Thy will, my God and the God of my fathers, not to let me fall into the hands of this angel." '

In Gnosticism the Apocryphon of John, found in the Nag Hammadi library, Old Cairo, Sama'el is the third name of the demiurge, whose other names are Saklas and Yaldabaoth. In this context, Sama'el means 'the blind god', in other words he was 'Ignorant of God above everything'. The theme of blindness readily occurs throughout Gnostic works.

To anthroposophists, Sama'el is known as one of the seven archangels: Saint Gregory identified Sama'el as one of the Angels of Creation together with; Mikh'ael, Gabri'el, Ana'el, Rapha'el, Orihi'el, and Zachari'el. All had a special assignment to act as Zeitgeist, or time spirits, each for periods of around three hundred and eighty years. Since the latter part of the nineteenth century anthroposophists imagined Mikh'ael to be the chief time spirit.

Four important archangels are also supposed to display periodic spiritual activity over the seasons: Rapha'el during spring, Mikh'ael during summer, Gabri'el during autumn and Uri'el during the winter.

In The Holy Kabbalah (Arthur Edward Waite, 255), Sama'el is described as the 'severity of God', and is listed as fifth of the archangels of the world of Briah. Sama'el is said to have taken Lil'ith as his bride after she left Adam. According to Zoharistic Cabala, Sama'el was also mated with Na'amah, Eisheth Zenunim, and Agrat Bat Mahlat — all angels of prostitution.

Sama'el appears as a strong muscular young man wearing a tunic on the style of the Romans with a flowing cloak. He has long red hair tied into a pony-tail. In his right hand he holds a short sword, fashioned in the Roman style. Some say on his breast is a bronze plate engraved with a pentagram. Sama'el has been described as one of the most beautiful of Archangels. Many of the Archangels are said to have six wings. Sama'el, like Metatron, is said to have twelve. He is also known as the most prominent 'Angel of Death' and is attributed to Mars.

Know this well – a negative sign of any planet does not mean a weak sign.

Here are some of the things the Angel Sama'el will help you with addition you may also petition on the following:

To recover physical strength after illness. To overcome enemies and help you fight the battles of life. To give physical courage. To help those in the armed forces especially soldiers. To help acquire the right machines you need and secure a good bargain.

In health matters He can be evoked for any ailment of the right arm, severe headaches, or to help in operations where He guides the surgeons hands and restores health quickly afterwards. He helps to heal all rashes and infections, and any ailments that cause eruptive spots. He safeguards you against risks of accidents from any kind of machinery.

Magical Intentions: Physical courage and overcoming enemies. Projects related to war - success, prevention and cause. Disrupts friendships and causes discord. The energies of this day best harmonize with efforts of masculine vibration, such as conflict, physical endurance and strength, lust, hunting, sports, and all types of competition. Use them, too, for rituals involving surgical procedures or political ventures. Courage, Physical Strength, Revenge, Military Honours, Surgery and the Breaking of Negative Spells, Matrimony, War, Enemies, Prison, Vitality and Assertiveness

Rulerships: Police matters, war, sports, engineering, machinery, male sexuality, surgery, physical strength, courage, protection, help in overthrowing enemies, aggression, ambition, arguments, competition, conflict, destruction, energy, goals, lust, medical issues, strife, struggle, upheaval, victory.

Negative aspects: Anger, violence.

The Angel Sama'el rules over two signs of the zodiac, Aries symbolized by the horns of the Ram ♈, and Scorpio, shown as the letter M with an arrow tipped tail ♏ this being the hieroglyph of a scorpion. Sama'el's planet Mars, is shown as an arrowed circle, for his private sign an upright sword, symbol of his protection of humanity from enemies and evil. Colours representative of Sama'el are: scarlet, orange and green.

Aries is the first sign or positive sign; Scorpio is the second or negative sign. Positive and negative signs have equal value, but different powers, just as people born under Aries and Scorpio have different characters, different but equal aspects of the same planet.

Throughout the pathworking many signs and symbolic forms will be revealed to you and it is important that you remember them, especially if you intend writing letters of petition.

When writing to this angel, draw his four symbols, write 'To Archangel Sama'el' in Passing the Rivers Script, the request in Theban Script and finally sign your secret name in Passing the Rivers Script.

ANGELIC MAGICK

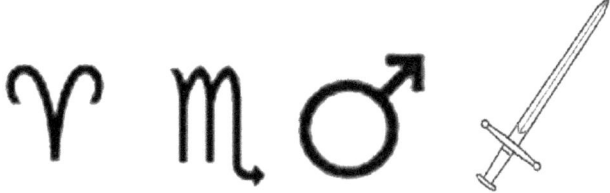

Letters to Archangel Sama'el must be written on a Tuesday at his appointed hour (see chart) using white paper and red ink. The day of writing counts as one day, kept for seven days and burnt on the following Tuesday.

Sama'el may use one or several of the signs during the course of the seven days, but one sign is enough to assume your request has been granted.

If you receive no sign from Sama'el, your request is refused. Magical help is not intended to take the place of your own efforts.

Magical letters can be written to any of the Ruling Angels but only on matters He rules, and on His day, you need to invoke or banish.

Do not complicate this system beyond what is given, as the letter is sufficient. Simplicity is the beauty of this art; the Voice of Angels is not a ritual system. So add the knowledge to what you already have and don't confuse systems.

> 'May the Archangel Sama'el grant
> and bless your request'

Path To Sama'el
'Venom of God'

What you will need:
Oil of frankincense, incense, charcoal, goblet of wine/beer, fruit juice or water, two red candles, a statue or picture of the angel (optional but very useful).

Preparation:
Don your white robe and tie an orange and red cord around your waist. This will be in respect for the Angel you will be working with. Anoint wrists, temples and throat with oil of frankincense. Light candles. Prepare charcoal and add incense as required. Fill goblet with liquid and raise it in salutation to the angels and place it back on your altar.

Sit comfortably in an upright chair and inhale very slowly and deeply. You are not just inhaling air, but joy, serenity, strength, vitality, courage, and whichever positive quality you want to affirm. Imagine the breath filling not only your lungs, but also the whole body – starting from the feet and culminating at a point between the eyebrows.

As you exhale not only do you expel carbon dioxide from your system, but also mental and emotional impurities such as weakness, discouragement and despair. Feel the intimate connection between the mind and the breath. Feel the flow of energy around your body as you prepare for your ritual working.

Say the temple prayer to the angels:

I call upon thy sacred name

Of the being that has been with me

Since the beginning of beginnings.

As I gaze upwards

May I behold thy beauty and thy splendour unto eternity,

Time without end.

Build your gate with love and care; visualise Angel Hair quartz crystal the colour of citrine pushing up through the earth, towering above your head and disappearing into the heavens. Visualise a brilliant shaft of light pass through it. Marvel at the smoky golden brown strands tipped with red sparks of colour as spirits dance within. The ten-edged crystal platform appears, but all suddenly changes to a dark grey colour as basalt magma erupts and fluid flows from vents that coalesce forming molten clots at your feet obliterating the yawning abyss below.

The air about you smells slightly of sulphur making you cough. You cup your hand over your nose and mouth, wondering where your guide is. The touch of a hand on your elbow makes you jump. Luc'ifer's amber colour eyes twinkle as he takes you by your right hand and indicates that you lead the way.

Fear and uncertainty rise up from your solar plexus and you tighten your grip on your guardian's hand. Reassured, together you walk clockwise around the perimeter of the platform and automatically you extend your left hand towards the molten mass and are surprised that it is cool to the touch, a shiver goes down your spine as ten crystal walls automatically erupt from the abyss and loom above. Inner voices ring out: 'All man is Divine' – feel the words within your heart.

Misty divine images of Mikh'ael and Gabri'el gaze knowingly at you, and through their crystal cells, they smile. You instinctively touch the glassy surface of the next cell and feel it dissolve beneath your fingertips. It is time to call forth the Archangel Sama'el.

Pause before beginning your invocation. Visualise each word as you utter it. Breathe it into life; endow it with passion and sincerity. Each is a rhythmic element combining to form a powerful symphony, imbue your call with such beauty that the angelic being cannot but help to respond. Not only will you be invoking Sama'el, but going on a journey into the centre of his realm. You will learn how to focus on his energy as you are drawn in. This is your gateway.

'Great Protector!

Warrior of God!

Defender of the elements of iron, bronze and brass,

Angel of teaching

Receive me into your realm.

Open my heart and my mind

That I may feel you, and know you.

Thou who resides in the Fifth Heaven Machon

Ruler of the Western and Southern Rivers,

I pray thee, show me a sign.'

The signature of the Archangel Sama'el ignites onto one of the cell walls.

Sama'el

sam-A-EL

Commit it to memory. This symbol is charged, look at each mark and take it within.

Spread before you are plains of molten lava flowing around the volcanic provinces of Tharsis and Elysium.

'What is this strange place?' you hear yourself say.

'It is Mars Pilgrim, and there are wondrous things to behold,' Luc'ifer says.

Yellow and white gases melt around you, cocooning your body. Tiny sparks of light bubble and squeak, as you lovingly touch them, saying:

'Come Spirits, within the glow of Mars,

Great Archangel of teaching

Brilliant art though who are ready to obey the power of the ancient tongue

Come assist me!

O Splendour of Tha-aoth

That which the Eternal Creator hath formed

I invoke thee.

In the Name of the beings who surround the Mighty Sama'el,

Thou who art the spirit of Counsel,

Thou who teacheth magic, and the science of law,

Be favourable, I pray thee.

Heavenly angel, guard me.'

Pause to allow your conscious mind to take in proceedings so far, let it become like a river flowing always towards enlightenment.

You are standing beneath the most ancient of trees, the Monkey Puzzle, its great body stretches to the red skies above. It is a living fossil amongst its brothers, Pilgrim. Beneath your feet are strewn the brown shells of the Horse Chestnut. The aroma of pepper is carried in a light breeze; joy fills you as wasps alight from thistles and nettles, their delicate wings brush against your cheeks. You marvel at the carpet of blood-red peonies that suddenly spring up around your feet attracting the great stinging insects and scorpions.

'I fear them not,

For thou Sama'el art with me.

Hail Great One!

Hail Sama'el!

Thee of the red giant.'

Stand proudly, shoulders squared, chin lifted with victorious pride.

Conjuration

I…. (utter your secret name) salute thee and conjure thee,

O beauteous Mars

O most beauteous Star

O light that reflects in my eyes

By the sulphur taste on my tongue

By the peppered air I breathe into my lungs,

I conjure thee.

By the names of the spirit princes living in you,

By the ineffable name on which created everything!

Thou who art responsible for the plants of blessedness

By the planet name of Ma'adim

By you, O resplendent One, appear!

Ruler of the Fifth Heaven Machon

Open my ears so that I may hear your sacred voice

Speak to me of thyself, so that I may learn more of thee.

Archangel Sama'el, appear before me

Grace my eyes with your presence!

An exhilarating smell of Cardamom, Catmint, Patchouli, and Carnation permeates the air. Drink in the aroma Pilgrim, and say:

'Bless-ed be He,

Bless-ed be the Archangel

Bless-ed be He

Hail Great One! Hail Sama'el!

Thou who now stands before me

O that I may look upon your wondrous face framed by long burnished red hair.

Strong and muscular is your form clad in a Roman toga of Royal Purple,

On your breastplate is emblazoned the seal of Mars

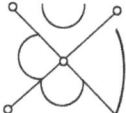

May I understand the meaning and take it within my heart.

I bow before thee

For thou art truly beautiful.'

In his right hand, Sama'el holds a short sword that he lifts in salutation to you. From his shoulders rise twelve wings, their bronze red feathers gently move in the gaseous air.

Scarlet-tinged clouds waft around you causing your skin on your right arm to tingle and itch. An apex in the atmosphere above your head opens and through it swoops Bartzabel the planetary demon; in bright sparks his black wings trace his sigil. The brilliant white aura around his chubby body highlights his shiny bald head and the clump black hair that springs from the nape of his thick neck. His black eyes twinkle in the magical light. Following closely in his wake is Graphi'el the planetary intelligence displaying his sigil in electric blue. Phaleg makes his entrance landing with a thud; his sigil is his footprint. They swagger around you; the nearness of them makes you shiver and recoil. Luc'ifer laughs and with a grand gesture they retreat back towards Sama'el.

Moments pass as ten pairs of eyes observe you. The silence is deafening – Sama'el speaks:

'I am known as the Angel of Death, do you not fear me Pilgrim?'

Think before you answer, Pilgrim:

'No, I do not fear you, as fear always springs from ignorance. I fear my lack of knowledge of you.'

Materialising before you is a bronze altar strewn with flowers and herbs. In the centre an iron brazier glows with red-hot coals and beside it a red glass vessel full of peppercorns, benzoin, tobacco leaf and dragon's blood.

Walk forward and take a handful of incense and cast it onto the burning coals and say:

'I pray thee Archangel Sama'el

Protector and gracious Angel Regent of Mars,

Receive these perfumed fumigations

May the rising flames from these herbs

Ignite my courage and send it into your realm.

I bow to thee Sama'el ever waiting and ever present,

Warrior of God, Great Archangel of Teaching,

I open my heart to you

And rejoice in your presence.'

Around you appear a ram leading a flock of sheep. The wool on the ram's back parts revealing the double-sided Kamea, tablet of Mars.

11	24	7	20	3
4	12	25	8	16
17	5	13	21	9
10	18	1	14	22
23	6	19	2	15

The numbers vibrate and impact upon your senses, feel the numbers within as they hum:

'Inside this square are divine names, Pilgrim, –of the Intelligence and Spirit -sacred to Sama'el through Mars.'

Sama'el beckons to Luc'ifer who strides forward and hugs his brother. The moment is special for them Pilgrim.

As they part, Luc'ifer turns around smiling, and hands you the sacred ring of Solomon.

Take the ring Pilgrim and put it on the index finger of your right hand.

A dazzling angelic being whose quivering halo coloured in every hue from red to gold, hovers above you dropping a crimson red silk tabard over your shoulders. Tiny flames ignite as it touches your skin. Feel the power and energy. Listen to voice of Sama'el.

'Ol gnonp prge aldi: lap zirdo
Sama'el casarm urbs oboleh grsam:'

'I garnish with the fire of gathering: for I am Sama'el Who beautified Your garments with admiration:'

It is at this stage where you may want to take some personal time with Sama'el for quiet introspection, conversation, meditation or whatever you need to build and cultivate your relationship with the archangel. Say:

'Odo cicle qaa. Odo ooaona arpuran Busdir.'

'Open my eyes so that I may see the First Glory.'

'Ia-Idon Sama'el Aao Ial- I Micma Adoian Mad

Soba Ooaona Chis Luciftias Piripsol'

'All-powerful Sama'el amongst the Flames

I behold the Face of your God

Whose Eyes are the Brightness of the Heavens.'

Around you there is a great shift through the volcanic crust, magma pours out and is neutralized solidifying into a network of channels filling red wax; The third rim of the Seal of Truth is revealed; heptagonal in shape.

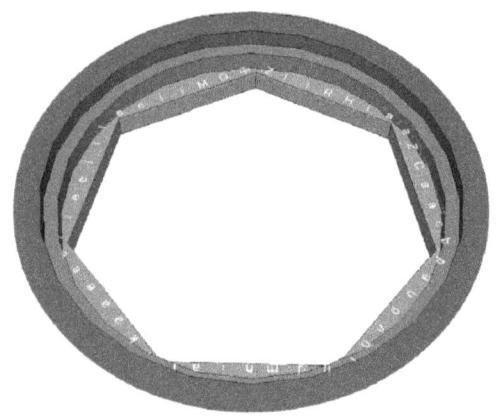

Luc'ifer indicates that you walk clockwise around the wax rims. The pressure of your footsteps causes arcs of brilliant light to flash within the ring illuminating symbolic images.

You turn around with a beseeching look at your guardian, who understands your confusion, but it is not he who answers, it is Uri'el, and again his voice travels along a lightning flash:

'Behold Pilgrim, we show you letters that represent the seven Seats of the One and everlasting Creator and Heavenly Son, and inwardly the Divine Spirit'

Pause Pilgrim, breath in these words that come from beyond, and be empowered:

'In the vital power of the human being

That which is ignited at birth

There glows that remembered image...'

The wax slowly melts and is absorbed back into the solidified magma leaving no trace of the seal. Take a deep breath and say:

'O divine one, Sama'el,

I thank thee!'

Your gratitude is interrupted by a high-pitch laugh shattering the moment. Through a scarlet red dust cloud a beautiful woman sidles towards Sama'el. Coiled around her naked form is an enormous snake. Sama'el turns abruptly from you in adoration for the woman, and says:

'Lil'ith, zylna piadph:
Abramg azien ta talho paracleda. Niiso! Lapzirdo mad.'

'Lil'ith, within the depth of my jaws: I have prepared my hands as cups for a wedding.

Come away! For I am your God.'

Your eyes widen in amazement, taking in the scene only for it to be obliterated by a viscous fluid that rises up like amorous arms enveloping Sama'el and Lil'ith, his bride.

Carbon dioxide and water vapor melt into a froth of gas bubbles producing glassy shards that erupt and explode about you. Luc'ifer however is not surprised by the events as he shields you from the blast, and indicates that it is time for you to leave the angelic realm of Sama'el.

Stand silently, and think about what you have uttered, what has been said to you and foremost, what has been revealed. Ask yourself Pilgrim: Has this experience changed me? Close your eyes and when you open them say these words:

'Eternal are the Archangels and Angels whose celestial realms endureth, forever and ever. I return thanks unto the Great Creator, in Whose Name thou, Sama'el hast come. Depart hence in peace unto thine habitations, and be thou ready to return when so ever I shall have need of thee.'

Utter your secret name to the angels, go through the portal into your world and seal the door behind you.

'May the Archangel Sama'el guard
and bless you and keep you safe'

5
Archangel Rapha'el
'God has healed'

Legend

Archangel Rapha'el is one of the most well known of the archangels. His name comes from the Hebrew word rapha'el or raphach, when translated, means 'God heals the soul'.

Rapha'el's origins can be traced back to the Mediterranean region before the time of Christ where he is included in a pantheon that had as the high god, El, his consort Atirat and her child, Rapha'el.

To the Greeks and Romans Rapha'el was their winged messenger god, Hermes or Mercury. Archangel Rapha'el belongs to the angelic choir of the Virtues, also known as 'the Shining' or 'Brilliant ones who heal'. The chief job of the Virtues is to provide miracles and blessings to humankind.

He is not only an angel of healing, but science and knowledge. He is the guardian of the Tree of Life in the Garden of Eden, angel of the sun and the angel of the evening winds. He is also a guide to the underworld.

Titles for which Archangel Rapha'el holds are; Angel of Love, Chief of the Guardian Angels, Ruler of the Sun, Angel of Heat, Prince of Virtues, Guardian of the Tree of Life, Angel of Sunday, Angel of Compassion, Angel of Force, Angel of the Melon

His symbol is the serpent or caduceus the well-known sign for healing in western medicine. Rapha'el is the patron saint of healers, writers, travellers, the blind and guardian of youth. Rapha'el is one of the six Angels of Repentance, Angel of Prayer, Love, Joy and Light.

According Louis Ginzberg in *Legend of the Jews,* Rapha'el's true name was Labbi'el and was a member of a group of angels, of which there were two, the 'angels of truth' and the 'angels of peace' who God destroyed by fire because they did not comply with the divine command to honour the creation of man. Labbi'el however, did comply, and his name was changed to Rapha'el.

He is one of the seven angels that attend the throne of God, and belongs to at least four of the celestial orders: seraphim, cherubim, dominions, and powers. Rapha'el appears to be the high archangel, according to Rabbi Abba in *The Zohar I,* charged to heal the earth, and through him…'the earth furnishes an abode for man, whom he heals of all ailments'.

He is not only known as the "angel who is set over all the diseases and all the wounds of the children of men, but Rapha'el has also been called 'a guide in hell,' who after all is where healing is needed the most.

He is often referred to in the Book of Enoch and although he is the archangel of healing, when necessary God uses him as a destroyer and warrior. In 1 Enoch 53.6 he is one of four angels together with Mikh'ael, Uri'el and Gabri'el who will cast Satan (Azazye'el) and his followers 'into a furnace of blazing fire, so that the Lord of spirits may be avenged of them for their crimes as they became ministers of Satan, and seduced those who dwell on earth'.

In the first Book of Enoch (second century BCE) talks about the Nephilim, 'sons of God', the children of the fallen angels referred to as 'the Watchers'. In anger, God sent Mikh'ael, Rapha'el and Gabri'el to bind the Watchers under the earth until Judgment Day.

It is claimed that it was Rapha'el who told Noah how to build the Ark and in another legend in the *Sefer Noah* that after the flood Rapha'el handed Noah a 'medical book' which may have been the famous *Sefer Razi'el (the Book of the Angel Razi'el).*

Indeed, Rapha'el's career seems to be occupied with medical missions. He is one of the three angels that visited Abraham in Genesis 18; the other two angels are usually identified as Gabri'el and Mikh'ael. Being the angel of healing God sent him to heal Abraham of the pain of circumcision. Abraham had neglected to observe this rite earlier in life and as an older man it was much harder on him.

In Gen: 32:24-25 God sent Rapha'el to cure Jacob of an injury to his thigh he received at Peni'el when he wrestled with his dark adversary, Sama'el. 'And Jacob was left alone; and a man (angel) wrestled with him until the breaking of the day. And when he (the angel) saw that he did not prevail against Jacob, he touched the hollow of his thigh; and Jacob's thigh was put out of joint as he wrestled with him…'

Rapha'el can be found in the Book of Tobit, a religious writing recognized by the Catholic and Orthodox Christian churches though not in the Hebrew Bible. Rapha'el is disguised as a human sent to help Tobias. The angel shows Tobias how to use parts of a fish he has caught, for healing. Tobias placed the gall bladder of the fish on his blind father's eyes and as a result the cataracts fell away, and his sight was restored.

One other story about this beautiful archangel is from *The Testament of Solomon*. Solomon prayed to God for help in building his Temple. God answered with the gift of a magic ring brought to the Hebrew king by Rapha'el. The ring was engraved with the pentacle (five-pointed star) that had the power to subdue all demons, and is believed that the slave labour of demons, Solomon was able to complete the building of the Temple.

Rapha'el is most often associated with healing or the rejuvenation of the mind, body and soul, the modern Hebrew word doctor of medicine is 'Rophe' connected to the same root word as Rapha'el.

Rapha'el is recognized by all three Abrahamic religions as an angel. However within Islam, he known as the archangel Israfel. Within Islamic scripture, the archangels Mikh'ael, Gabri'el and Azrael usually accompany Israfel. As stated within the Hadith (narrations relating to the words and deeds of the prophet Mohammad) Israfel was given the task of blowing into a large horn signalling Judgement Day.

Rapha'el is possibly the most widely recognized and appealing of the seven archangels. He is frequently depicted in Western art; his image is featured on the canvases of masters such as Botticelli, Titian, and Rembrandt. In Christian paintings he is portrayed carrying a pilgrim's stick, a wallet and a fish.

Rapha'el is one of many heavenly beings featured in John Milton's 17th century epic poem entitled *Paradise Lost*. In this literary work Rapha'el is commanded by God to remind Adam about the deadly sin involved with partaking from the Tree of the knowledge of good and evil. Obviously as the Old Testament story goes, Adam does eat of the forbidden fruit or apple, therefore leaving Rapha'el's advice by the wayside.

Magical Intention: He oversees matters of business, trade, job change and gaining employment, and the will to succeed. The Angel Rapha'el above all rules thought and mental inspiration, and as thought and inspiration are virgin in that they are productive without the need of a father. Thought is conceived in the mind of one, and so is a virgin. Inspiration means 'spirit in dwelling' and so it is truly an 'immaculate conception' of the virgin thoughts, hence the ♍ sign of the planet mercury is named Virgo. The birth of anything created must first begin as thought, though it may be enhanced by inspiration, or improved by spirit. Influencing people, theatre, mental ability and gifted speaking. Wednesday's vibration adds power to rituals involving inspiration, poets, writers, communications, the written and spoken word, and all matters of study, learning, and teaching. Today is a good time to begin efforts involving self-improvement or understanding.

Colours representative of him are yellow and light blue.

Rulership: To brighten and invigorate the mind, strengthen concentration and inspiration, healing lung and chest complaints, and ailments of the left arm and hand. He aids and preserves health generally, particularly that of children. He oversees road, rail, or air travel, commerce, healing, the media, mathematics, science, industry, intelligence, eloquence, and prophesy, business, buying and selling, cleverness, communication, contracts, creativity, information, memory, perception, science, wisdom, writing.

Signs: A gift of a mirror or, for a mirror to cloud over. If you break a mirror accidentally, it *does not* employ bad luck, especially if you have written to the Angel Rapha'el, it is a god omen as mirrors are backed with silver or mercury, the metal of this angel.

Negative aspects: dishonesty, deception.

Rapha'el is the Angel of Mercury – Zodiacal signs Gemini being positive and Virgo being negative. Gemini is represented by the Roman numeral ♊ signifying the twins. Virgo is shown by the letter ♍ with a closed loop on the edge of the ♍, this represents the virgin aspect of the goddess; the loop signifies the closed or crossed legs of the virgin symbolizing purity.

A bird's head is used as the Angel Rapha'el's own sign likened to the ancient Egyptian's Thoth, the Ibis headed god, as Rapha'el is one of the angels of the air and the air is the natural element of birds. He also symbolizes thoughts flying across the sky of the mind. Rapha'el's methods are swift like birds in flight. Any bird head is Rapha'el.

Throughout the pathworking many signs and symbolic forms will be revealed to you and it is important that you remember them, especially if you intend writing letters of petition.

When writing to this angel, draw his four symbols, write 'To Archangel Rapha'el' in Passing the River Script, and the request in Theban Script and finally sign your secret name in Passing the River Script.

Letters to the Angel Rapha'el must be written on a Wednesday according to the appropriate hour of that day (see chart) using green paper and black ink, the letter is kept for seven days – Wednesday to Wednesday – then burnt.

Rapha'el may use one or several of the signs during the course of the seven days, but one sign is enough to assume your request has been granted.

If you receive no sign from Rapha'el, your request has been refused. Magical help is not intended to take the place of your own efforts.

Magical letters can be written to any of the Ruling Angels but only on matters He rules, and on His day, you need to invoke or banish.

Do not complicate this system beyond what is given the letter is sufficient. Simplicity is the beauty of this art; the Voice of Angels is not a ritual system. So add the knowledge to what you already have and don't confuse systems.

> 'May the Archangel Rapha'el grant
> and bless your request'

Path to Rapha'el

What you will need:
Oil of frankincense, incense, charcoal, goblet of wine/beer, fruit juice or water, two yellow candles, a statue or picture of the angel (optional but very useful).

Preparation:
Don your white robe and tie a yellow and light blue cords around your waist. This will be in respect for the Angel you will be working with. Anoint wrists, temples and throat with oil of frankincense. Light candles. Prepare charcoal and add incense as required. Fill goblet with liquid and raise it in salutation to the angels and place it back on your altar.

Sit comfortably in an upright chair and inhale very slowly and deeply. You are not just inhaling air, but joy, serenity, strength, vitality, courage, and whichever positive quality you want to affirm. Imagine the breath filling not only your lungs, but also the whole body – starting from the feet and culminating at a point between the eyebrows.

As you exhale not only do you expel carbon dioxide from your system, but also mental and emotional impurities such as weakness, discouragement and despair. Feel the intimate connection between the mind and the breath. Feel the flow of energy around your body as you prepare for your ritual working.

Say the temple prayer to the angels:

I call upon thy sacred name

Of the being that has been with me

Since the beginning of beginnings.

As I gaze upwards

May I behold thy beauty and thy splendour unto eternity,

Time without end.

Build your gate with love and care; visualise Angel Hair quartz crystal the colour of citrine pushing up through the earth, towering above your head and disappearing into the heavens. Visualise a brilliant shaft of light pass through it. Marvel at the smoky golden brown strands tipped with red sparks of colour as spirits dance within. The ten-edged crystal platform beneath your feet turns to the colour of slate obscuring the abyss below.

You are alone and wonder where Luc'ifer, your guardian can be. The edge of the platform begins to hum; what is it trying to tell you? Instinct makes you walk clockwise round the perimeter tracing a line through the air with your left hand. The atmosphere splits as ten crystal walls erupt from the abyss and tower above. Inner voices ring out: 'All man is Divine' – feel the words within your heart.

'I've done it!' you hear yourself say.

You readily recognize the three archangels within their individual cells, Mikh'ael, Gabri'el and Sama'el; again their eyes shine forth upon you. As you touch the fifth cell wall it softens and you feel a current of energy pulsing from within.

'It is time to call forth the Archangel Rapha'el, Pilgrim.' Your heart is gladdened knowing that Luc'ifer is again by your side.

Pause before beginning your invocation. Visualise each word as you utter it. Breathe it into life; endow it with passion and sincerity. Each is a rhythmic element combining to form a powerful symphony, imbue your call with such beauty that the angelic being cannot but help to respond. Not only will you be invoking Rapha'el, but going on a journey into the centre of his realm. You will learn how to focus on his energy as you are drawn in. This is your gateway.

'Messenger of the Gods!

Defender of the element of air,

Angel of Healing,

Angel of Prayer, Love, Joy and Light

Thou who stands in the presence of God,

Ruler of the Cherubim,

Seraphim, Dominions, and Powers, and

Divine protector of children,

Receive me into your realm.

Open my heart and my mind

That I may feel you, and know you.

Thou who art Ruler of the First Heaven

Watcher of the North and East,

I pray thee, show me a sign.'

An unseen hand writes Archangel Rapha'el on one of the cell walls.

Rapha'el

Raf- A –EL.

Commit it to memory. This symbol is charged, look at each mark and take it within. From the skies above meteorites pelt down towards you but friction instantly burns them up. It is extremely hot and almost airless with very little gravity. A solar wind gently carries you forward. This is Mercury, and around you are signs and symbols of Rapha'el. Take a deep breath and say:

'Come, Spirits adorned in the power of Mercury,

Radiant Spirits who are ready to obey the power of the ancient tongue,

Come assist me in the operation that I am making.

With the aid of the Majestic light

O Splendour of Gethog

That which the Eternal Creator hath formed

I invoke thee for these purposes.

I pray thee, be favourable to what I shall ask.

In the Name of the beings who surround and reflect the Mighty Rapha'el,

Heavenly angel, guard me.'

You slowly descend and as you touch the surface the grey-cratered earth cracks, pushing forth, bright yellow flowers, ferns, brackens and leafy green weeds. From further cracks spring Aspine's and Silver Birch; small monkeys chatter and spring from branch to branch, shaking tiny mirrors that adorn the trees; their light casting a myriad of lights around you. On a branch hangs a golden cage, and within it is a beautiful bird; its happy chattering echoes through the air. Ibis strut around you, their long black beaks snatch at a swarm of flies.

'Hail Rapha'el!

I thank thee for these magical signs.

Around me is heady scent of Sandalwood, Narcissus and Cinnamon.

With each intake of breath,

May the tangy smell of Verbena and warmth of Chamomile fill my lungs.

I pray that these aromas serve to intensify my awareness of thee.'

Pause to allow your conscious mind to take in events so far, let it become like a mirror, reflecting, but allowing light through the stillness of the silver-white skies above.

Conjuration

I ….. (utter your secret name) salute thee and conjure thee,

O beautiful Mercury,

O most beautiful Planet,

By the thin air that surrounds me,

By the strange gases around me,

By the names of the spirit princes living in you,

By the ineffable name on which created everything!

By the planet name of KVKB

By you, O resplendent One, appear!

Ruler of the Second Heaven Ra-quia

I conjure thee.

Grace my eyes with your presence

Archangel Rapha'el, appear before me!

Beneath your feet are smooth plains and many deep craters similar to those on the moon; craters that were formed when meteors and small comets crashed into the planet. The scent of Lavender, Marjoram and Lilly of the Valley is all around you. Drink in the aroma Pilgrim, and say:

Bless-ed be He,

Bless-ed be the Archangel

Bless-ed be He

Hail Great One! Hail Rapha'el!

Thou who now stands before me

Thou whose face is youthful and filled with serenity

Golden is your hair.

Of palest blue are your eyes,

Those lips like rose petals

O that they may speak words so precious

O that my ears alone will hear your voice.

Youthful is your delicate form clad in yellow flowing robes,

Powerful is the eight-pointed star that hangs from your fine neck,

Gentle is your right hand that carries the caduceus,

Mark of healing.

Magnificent is the quick darting light penetrating the gases around your form

The light of which forms the talisman above your head

I pray that I shall know its meaning and take it within my heart.

I, the Pilgrim stand before you enthralled,

May the tenderness of your spirit rest within my soul.'

The heavens light up. Around you fall meteorites hitting the ground so fiercely they split open revealing first Taph-thart-harath, the planetary spirit and ethereal soul of Mercury, and glowing yellow within his breast, his sigil . Tiri'el, Mercury's planetary intelligence emerges from the second meteorite charging the atmosphere around him with his sigil . Luc'ifer is beside himself with excitement and rushes towards Rapha'el who hugs him affectionately, and says:

'Ol brint aai, Luc'ifer. Yls brin ip teloah. Niis esiasch, bliorax hoath Iaida.'

'I have been amongst you, Lucifer. Thou hast not been dead to me. Come my brother, let us comfort this true worshiper of the Highest.'

The coiled serpent from the caduceus in Rapha'el's right hand, slithers away from the archangel and moves towards you. Be not afraid Pilgrim, not only is the serpent the sign of healing, but also of great wisdom. Its body slides across your feet leaving a trickle of mercury in its wake. The liquid solidifies into the double-sided Kamea. The hissing serpent returns to his master.

8	58	59	5	4	62	63	1
49	15	14	52	53	11	10	56
41	23	22	44	45	19	18	48
32	34	35	29	28	38	39	25
40	26	27	37	36	30	31	33
17	47	46	20	21	43	42	24
9	55	54	12	13	51	50	16
64	2	3	61	60	6	7	57

You hear a voice say:

'Within this square are divine names, Pilgrim, of the Intelligence and Spirit of Spirits – sacred to Rapha'el through Mercury.'

At your right side is an aluminium table holding a dish of incense and a brazier filled with burning coals take a handful of incense and cast it onto the coals and say:

'I pray thee Archangel Rapha'el

Healer and gracious angel of Mercury,

Receive these perfumed fumigations

May the rising flames from these herbs

Ignite my courage and send it into your realm.

I bow to thee Rapha'el,

Angel of Heat, Prince of Virtues and Guardian of the Tree of Life,

I open my heart to you

And rejoice in your presence.'

It is at this stage where you may want to take some personal time with Rapha'el for quiet introspection, conversation, meditation or whatever you need to build and cultivate your relationship with the archangel.

Luc'ifer walks forward holding the sacred ring of Solomon and crimson red silk tabard. Take the ring Pilgrim, put it on the index finger of your right hand, put the tabard over your shoulders, and say:

'I feel the power from these sacred objects rise within me,

I feel my minds eye open

Thus I am ready O Great and Divine Being,

May that I know more of the Seal of Truth

Great Archangel Rapha'el I pray thee,

'Odo cicle qaa.
Odo ooaona arpuran Pirgah.'

'Open the Mysteries of Your Creation.
Open my eyes so that I may see the sacred.'

A flutter of wings disturbs the air in front of you, and appears a sole angel proffering you a plate full of ripe mulberries. You extend your hand to take a juicy fruit that brings a smile to the lips of Rapha'el, who says:

'Pilgrim, thou art hungry for knowledge.'

Like soft rain wax gently falls from the heavens and solidifies into a system of steps on the ground before you. Archangel Rapha'el points his caduceus at the wax, burning more letters into the rims, and utters:

'Aleph-Mem-Tav. Behold more
of the mystery of the Seal of Truth is revealed.'

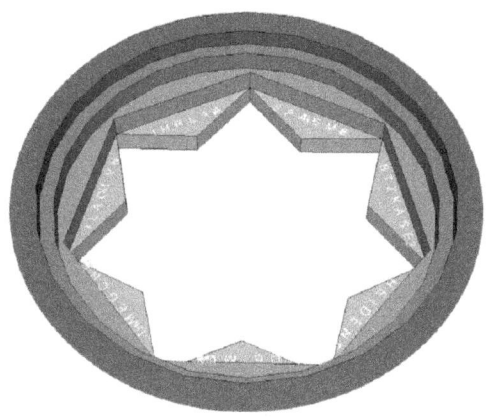

Wave after wave of names impact upon your senses, and just inside the arcs are written sacred names, the words dissolve into forty-nine notes that rebound around the rim ricocheting from the heptagon edge creating lightning flashes. Take a deep breath Pilgrim and absorb these energy sounds into the core of your being as they represent the Seven Angels who stand before the presence of the Great Creator.

The atmosphere around you suddenly warms causing the wax steps to melt away. The dark sky above fills you with strange melancholy as you stand alone on a landscape of grey-cratered rock and wonder what it is all about; so many symbols, and those haunting beautiful sounds. You reflect on what you have uttered, what has been said to you and foremost, what has been revealed. Ask yourself Pilgrim: Has this experience changed me?

Instinct tells you it is time to leave the angelic realm of Rapha'el. Close your eyes and when you open them say these words:

'Eternal are the Archangels and Angels whose celestial realms endureth, forever and ever. I return thanks unto the Great Creator, in Whose Name thou, Rapha'el hast come. Depart hence in peace unto thine habitations, and be thou ready to return when so ever I shall have need of thee.'

Utter your secret name to the angels, go through the portal into your world and seal the door behind you.

>'May the Archangel Rapha'el guard
>and bless you and keep you safe'

6
Archangel Zadki'el
'Righteousness of God'

Legend

Zadki'el (Tzadqi'el in Hebrew 'Righteousness of God') also known as Sachi'el, Zedeki'el, Zadaki'el, Tzadki'el, Zedekul and Hesedi'el. He is an archangel of the order of Cherubim, the Hasmallim and Dominions, who are all closely linked. The Dominions displayed such devotion to the Great Creator, they were chosen as the first angels to be given free will to control the universe without supervision. In other words, Zadlki'el is the archangel that watches over all the duties of the entire host of angels, *and* the universe!

Zadki'el is an angel of justice who ranks fourth among the ten Archangels of the Briatic (Kabbalistic) world. In Halachic Midrashim 11 (study of scripture) records him among the angels who guard the gates of the East Wind.

According to the Great Creators design, particular angels such as Zadki'el was a controller and organizer of the highest level and would not have appeared to the prophets, he would have in turn sent other angels to answer man's call.

He is in charge of the fifth heaven and as one of the princes of the seven heavens (Third Book of Enoch) he is attended by 496,000 myriads of ministering angels.

In Maseket Azilut, Zadki'el is listed as co-chief with Gabri'el of the order of Shinanim (Psalms 1 xviii. 18). As an angel of mercy, some texts claim that Zadki'el was said to be the Angel who prevented Abraham from sacrificing his son Isaac, and for this reason Zadki'el is usually shown holding a dagger.

When it comes to artistic imagery there are many beautiful paintings of the archangel Zadki'el such as Rembrandt's imagery dramatically illustrating the story of the faith of Abraham. The Angel Zadki'el grasps and holds back the hand of the patriarch, and startled, Abraham drops his knife. Rembrandt encapsulates a brief moment and freezes the action in mid air.

Zadki'el is often associated with the colour purple or violet, and hence most of the paintings that feature the angel are bright and colourful. In many of these paintings that exist, some of which are earlier period pieces from centuries past, Zadki'el will be seen wearing a long flowing violet coloured robe and sash, holding a flaming sword, and having outstretched pure white angelic wings.

Orthodox Jews hold the belief that the archangel Zadki'el as a warrior angel along with Jophi'el, are two mighty standard bearers who follow the archangel Mikh'ael each time he marches into battle. Along with Mikh'ael and Jophi'el, Zadki'el helped cast Luc'ifer out of heaven.

 Many Jewish and Christian scholars share this belief, that makes Zadki'el and official canonical scripture backed archangel, which is important because many of the archangels originate from non-canonical scripture such as the Book of Enoch.

Throughout Jewish literature recognizes Zadki'el's angelic expertise affecting mankind is mercy, freedom, compassion, benevolence and the Patron angel of all who forgive. Zadki'el gives us the ability to see beyond our earth-based perceptions of our relationships and to appreciate that true relationships transcend this earthly experience. This allows us to gain appreciation for the spiritual journey and the ability to find peace, harmony and especially forgiveness on the path that each of us shares with others.

This angel has a kind and gentle presence whose energy is supreme compassion that naturally aligns us with the ability to see and experience the divine aspect within us all. Zadki'el's mission is to release mankind from the burden of 'unhealed' energy that we have not only held against 'the self', but against others.

This angel guards the powers of invocation, and the best known and most powerful form, is prayer. We can pray to this sacred one for comfort when we are in need of gentle guidance. Zadki'el also stimulates a desire for spiritual development in humankind.

Magical Intentions: The achievement of general ambitions, health and wealth. He generates friendships and social prestige, governs lawyers, legal affairs and justice. Zadki'el's day is Thursday, and the vibrations of this day attune well to all matters involving material gain. Use them for working rituals that entail general success, accomplishment, honours and awards, or legal issues. These energies are also helpful in matters of luck, gambling, and prosperity. He is called upon to help reverse negativity in thought and deed and to open the mind to true perceptions. He can be invoked to grant the requestor a good memory. It is claimed that if a prayer or summoning is conducted to draw out Zadki'el's power, it can be aimed at someone whose heart is full of vengeance, and once touched by the archangel's holy essence, they will let go of their grudge or ill will. In some magic rituals one can bind Zadki'el's power or mercy with a small piece of amethyst, the crystal is then given as a necklace or bracelet to the person harbouring un-forgiveness or a grievance against the magic spell's binder.

Zadki'el, like all those within the Angelic Realm, will come with unconditional love, providing guidance and assistance towards our highest good and always honoring our Free Will.

Rulerships: His rulership extends to all money affairs, legal matters of judgement, be it your own or another's, social life, and securing the aid of people in power or supreme social position. In health matters he heals complaints caused by impure blood or bad circulation, ailments of the right leg, illness of both ankles and feet, and varicose veins. He helps in wage rises and brings better monetary conditions together.

Other signs sacred to him are receiving a gift of a fish, whale or elephant, or see them unexpectedly, a sudden trip to the sea or a boat trip, news of a visit from a sailor or fisherman, any gift connected with the sea, or from the seaside.

Negative aspects: Greed, wastefulness.

The Angel Zadki'el rules Sagittarius shown as an arrow ♐. This is the positive sign and Pisces, the two fish ♓, his negative sign. The sigil of his planet is Jupiter ♃, similar in shape to the number 4, and is the hieroglyph for the beard of Zeus and the Royal Swan. Zadki'el's private sign represents the expansion of fortune, and all good things, which is why it appears on many money talismans. All these are used to head the letters to this archangel. Colours representative of him are purple and royal blue.

Throughout the pathworking many signs and symbolic forms will be revealed to you and it is important that you remember them, especially if you intend writing letters of petition.

When writing to this angel draw his four symbols, then write 'To Archangel Zadki'el'. Magical letters to him should be written throughout, including your secret name, in Passing of Rivers Script. The colours are purple ink on white paper, or blue ink on lavender colour paper.

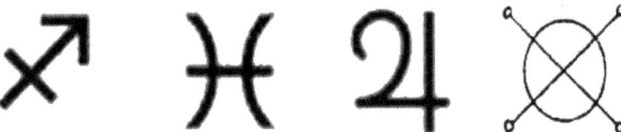

The letters must be written on a Thursday at his appointed hour (see chart) kept for seven days, and burnt on the following Thursday. The day of writing counts as one day.

Zadki'el may use one or several of the signs during the course of the seven days, but one sign is enough to assume your request has been granted. Should you not receive any sign, do not repeat your letters until seven days have elapsed. Signs will not be given to you until the time is right.

Magical letters can be written to any of the Ruling Angels but only on matters He rules, and on His day, you need to invoke or banish.

Do not complicate this system beyond what is given, as the letter is sufficient. Simplicity is the beauty of this art, the Voice of Angels is not a ritual, add the knowledge to what you already have and don't confuse systems.

'May the Archangel Zadki'el grant
and bless your request'

Path to Zadki'el

What you will need:
Oil of frankincense, incense, charcoal, goblet of wine/beer, fruit juice or water, two purple candles, a statue or picture of the angel (optional but very useful).

Preparation:
Don your white robe and tie a purple cord around your waist. This will be in respect for the Angel you will be working with. Anoint wrists, temples and throat with oil of frankincense. Light candles. Prepare charcoal and add incense as required. Fill goblet with liquid and raise it in salutation to the angels and place it back on your altar.

Sit comfortably in an upright chair and inhale very slowly and deeply. You are not just inhaling air, but joy, serenity, strength, vitality, courage, and whichever positive quality you want to affirm. Imagine the breath filling not only your lungs, but also the whole body – starting from the feet and culminating at a point between the eyebrows.

As you exhale not only do you expel carbon dioxide from your system, but also mental and emotional impurities such as weakness, discouragement and despair. Feel the intimate connection between the mind and the breath. Feel the flow of energy around your body as you prepare for your ritual working.

Say the temple prayer to the angels:

I call upon thy sacred name

Of the being that has been with me

Since the beginning of beginnings.

As I gaze upwards

May I behold thy beauty

And thy splendour unto eternity,

Time without end.

Build your gate with love and care; visualise Angel Hair quartz crystal the colour of citrine pushing up through the earth, towering above your head and disappearing into the heavens. Visualise a brilliant shaft of light pass through it. Marvel at the smoky golden brown strands tipped with red sparks of colour as spirits dance within. A portal opens for you; it is made of solid ammonia. Rain-like droplets of helium and neon precipitate downward through finger-like crystals. Ultra-violet light floods the portal illuminating your white robe intensifying the vibrant purple of your sash.

You are suddenly very hot. It is the thermal radiation produced from the atmosphere of Jupiter! You instantly look down knowingly, yes below you is the abyss, and yes, you are standing on the ten-edged crystal platform. You are alone and your guardian is nowhere to be seen. A voice inside your head tells you to open the way. Trace a line through the air with your left hand. Zones are formed; elongated cells of crystallized ammonia burst through the floor of the platform sending vaporous clouds that mask everything from your view.

'All man is Divine.' Your utterance of these words materializes Luc'ifer, who tumbles forth, falling at your feet. You offer your hand to help him up but he has already pulled himself from the gaseous floor and is also touching the sixth cell on the crystal wall with his index finger of his right hand.

'Begin your invocation Pilgrim! Bring forth Zadki'el the perfect one.' Luc'ifer orders you. 'Visualise each word as you utter it. Breathe it into life Pilgrim; endow it with passion and sincerity. Each is a rhythmic element combining to form a powerful symphony, imbue your call with such beauty that the angelic being cannot but help to respond. Not only will you be invoking Zadki'el, but going on a journey into the centre of his realm. You will learn how to focus on his energy as you are drawn in. This is your gateway!'

'Patron angel of all who forgive!

Defender of the element of fire and water,

Angel of compassion,

Divine angel of mercy,

Receive me into your realm.

Open my heart and my mind

That I may feel you, and know you.

Thou who art Ruler of the Sixth Heaven, Zebul.

Ruler of the West and South,

Guardian of the East Wind

I pray thee, show me a sign.'

Slowly the signature of the Archangel Zadki'el appears on to the cell wall.

Zadki'el

zad- KI- EL

Commit it to memory. This symbol is charged, look at each mark and take it within. A turbulent storm erupts causing a great red spot to appear, the glow reaches out past the edge of the planet where around it circles sixty-three moons, each pulsates a vivid colour. The moons of Thebe and Amalthea move around the giant planet, in the outer gossamer ring their opalescent halos throb with an inner light. Luc'ifer too looks up at the spectacle, his face serene but a touch of sorrow in his amber coloured eyes.

Raise your hands and say:

'Come Spirits,

Radiant Spirits who are ready to obey the power of the ancient tongue,

Great Archangel of Jupiter

Come assist me!

O Splendour of Gethog that which the Eternal Creator hath formed

I invoke thee!

In the Name of the beings who surround the Mighty Zadki'el,

Thou who art the spirit of Mercy,

Great teaching angel

Be favourable, I pray thee.

Heavenly angel, guard me.'

A giant Royal Oak tree has grown before you; its branches are knotted and knarled with age. More trees appear; Chestnut, Norway Spruce, Fig, Beech and Poplar. A heady smell brings a visiting Queen bee to inspect lilac bushes; their deep purple flower bunches hang lazily around you. Clumps of narcissus and poppies, their colourful flowers compete for the Queen bee's attention. Their colour contrasts with the delicate paper-like white leaves of honesty plants.

'Hail Zadki'el

I thank thee for showing me these signs,

I pray that with all I perceive

May it serve to deepen my understanding of thee.'

Pause to allow your conscious mind to take in events so far, let it become like a beacon, filled with the mightiness that surrounds you.

Conjuration
I ….. (utter your secret name) salute thee and conjure thee,

O beautiful Jupiter,

O most beautiful Planet,

By the sacred light that shines about me

By the names of the spirit princes living in you

I conjure thee.

By the ineffable name on which created everything!

By you, O resplendent One, appear!

And by the planet name of TzDQ

Ruler of the Sixth Heaven Zebul

I conjure thee.

Open my ears so that I may hear your sacred voice

Speak to me of thyself, so that I may learn more of thee.

Grace my eyes with your presence

Archangel Zadki'el appear before me!'

'May you be blessed.' Luc'ifer takes your right hand and presses a coin and a shiny acorn into your palm. You close you hand over the objects, and when you open it, a tiny money spider falls from your fingers.

The atmosphere around you is filled with a purple haze and within it dart tiny orbs of golden light, as they gently touch your body, haunting sounds ring out. Say:

'Bless-ed be He,

Bless-ed be the Archangel

Bless-ed be He

Hail Great One! Hail Zadki'el!

Thou who now stands before me

The hair framing your old face is the colour of bright shining steel

Aged is the hand that holds the jewelled sceptre

Encrusted with Amethysts,

It dazzles me.

I behold a robe of Royal purple,

And a flowing cloak of darkest blue that parts, and

Shining forth in a light so splendid, I perceive the seal of Jupiter

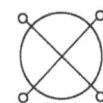

I pray that I shall know its meaning

And realize the visions within.

I bow before thee

For thou art the sole watcher over the universe.'

From within the halo of the moon Thebes drift three angelic beings. So beautiful is the display, you cup your hands against your chest in wonder. Misty strands of ether form around you as Bethor the Olympic spirit emerges, saying:

'Thou art empowered Pilgrim.'

His voice showers you with golden sparks forming his wondrous sigil . Hisma'el follows; his sparks fall, and on your right hand forms the sigil of his spirit .

Moment's pass – Jophi'el drifts towards you and presents his sigil, , and says:

'I am the Intelligence of Jupiter.'

The sparks dissolve into your hand and the feeling is wonderful, generating a strange tingling sensation down your right leg.

The screech of an eagle alerts you to an offering table in front of you. Garlands of buttercups, carnation, lobelia, sweet-scented pink valerian and purple heliotrope decorate the edge.

On the table are pumpkin seeds, a sprig of thyme and bunches of plump purple grapes; some have split open, their juices slowly ooze out. In the centre is a brazier of burning coals and a tin dish filled with nutmeg, cinnamon, cloves, cedar, saffron, and pomegranate seeds.

Archangel Zadki'el's soft lips curve in a smile. He extends his sceptre creating voluminous grey clouds that separate, exposing the double-sided Kamea.

4	14	15	1
9	7	6	12
5	11	10	8
16	2	3	13

What do they mean? You hear yourself say. They vibrate and impact upon your senses, feel the numbers within as they hum:

'Inside this square are divine names, Pilgrim, of the Intelligence and Spirit – sacred to Zadki'el through Jupiter.'

Walk forward and take a handful of incense and cast it onto the burning coals and say:

'I pray thee Archangel Zadki'el

Gracious angel of justice.

Receive these perfumed fumigations

May the rising flames from these herbs

Ignite my courage and send it into your realm.

I bow to thee Zadki'el who is ever waiting and ever-present,

Thou who whose energy is supreme compassion

I open my heart to you

And rejoice in your presence.'

Zadki'el looks long and hard at Luc'ifer, the expression in his eyes reflects a time when he and his brother Mikh'ael expelled this angel from heaven.

'Solpeth bien, Luc'ifer.'

'Hearken unto my voice Luc'ifer.'

Luc'ifer bows low as Zadki'el continues:

'Gmacalzo: Soba aath trian Luiahe,
Odecrin de mad aqlo qaaon.'

'In power and presence: Whose works shall be a Song of Honour,
And the praise of your God. In your creation.'

Zadki'el softens his manner and stretches out his arms and gathers up his brother Luc'ifer, holding him close to his broad chest.

'Come Luc'ifer, let us regale our Pilgrim as befits the initiate.'

The sacred ring of Solomon and a crimson silk tabard is produced. You take them, saying:

'These I take and wear with honour

I feel the power and energy rise within me.'

It is at this stage where you may want to take some personal time with Zadki'el for quiet introspection, conversation, meditation or whatever you need to build and cultivate your relationship with the archangel. Say:

'Drilpa Pir Zadki'el, mirc Othilrit
Zamran pambt hoath Iaida
Odo ooaona arpuran Pirgah.'

'Great Archangel Zadk'i'el upon the Seat of Mercy
Show me the true worshipper of The Highest
Open my eyes so that I may see the sacred.'

Many eyes are upon you.

'Are you ready Pilgrim?' Archangel Zadki'el asks.

'I am ready.' You affirm.

The stars reign down bringing with them a shower of wax that quickly forms five steps, shapes of intertwined heptagrams, all descend into nothingness. It mesmerizes you as you stare into infinite layers of chaos; an aligned plane of existence.

'What do you see, Pilgrim?' Luc'ifer enquires.

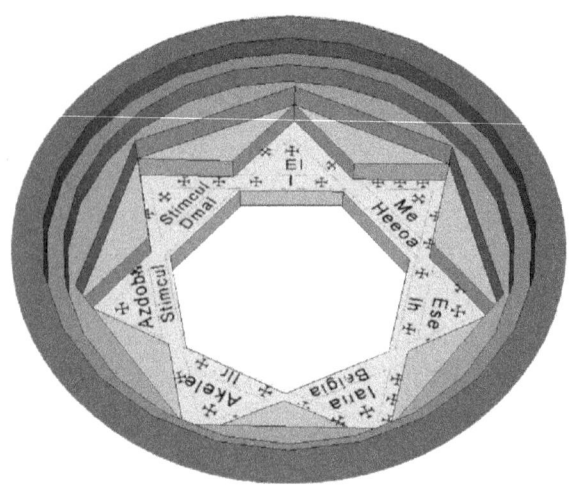

Moments pass. You reply:

'I see veiled shapes that appear to resemble human form, and each one contains a body of light that dazzles me.'

Pause Pilgrim, breath in the words you are about to utter, be empowered by them, and say:

'Between these God-names and the Planetary Angels in this sigil are four extra ranks of beings, they appear to be outside the realm of the Archangels!'

Zadki'el and Luc'ifer nod with approval and indicate that you continue.

'They say they are the 'children' of the Archangels.' As you speak, the visions raise their heads, and with a combined look, made of sweet accord, they gaze right into your very soul. Within this space and time, one comes forward speaking words of pure sound and light:

'Pilgrim, through me, a Son in flesh and in Spirit, the Divine Being has predicted eternal Heaven. There will come a time in the not too distant future, when there will be obtained the everlasting pattern in creation of organized sharing. Even though we are outside the Archangels realm, and most likely superior to them, this pattern of sharing is the master plan for all of us Sons and Daughters of the Creator. We are chosen to go out into space and meet together in an attempt to duplicate in time, the central universe of eternal perfection.'

The words 'central universe of eternal perfection' rebound around the edges of the seal creating multiple tones that ring about you. Guard this moment and keep it within. As you turn and walk back up the steps the wax melts back into the ground leaving no trace of the sigil or the apparitions.

Luc'ifer takes you by your hand, holding it briefly; Zadki'el raises his amethyst-jewelled sceptre, bestowing a blessing upon you.

Pilgrim, reflect on what you have uttered, what has been said to you and foremost, what has been revealed. Ask yourself: 'Has this experience changed me?'

Luc'ifer tells you it is time to leave the angelic realm of Zadki'el. Close your eyes and when you open them say these words:

'Eternal are the Archangels and Angels whose celestial realms endureth, forever and ever. I return thanks unto the Great Creator, in Whose Name thou, Zadki'el hast come. Depart hence in peace unto thine habitations, and be thou ready to return when so ever I shall have need of thee.'

Utter your secret name to the angels, go through the portal into your world and seal the door behind you.

'May the Archangel Zadki'el guard
and bless you and keep you safe'

7
Archangel Ana'el
'Joy of God'

Legend

The name Hani'el or Ana'el (the name we will be using) probably derives from Hebrew *hana'ah*, 'joy', 'pleasure', all qualities associated with the planet Venus, plus the suffix –el, 'God'. He may also be known as Hana'el , Hami'el, Onoel, or Ani'el. His name means 'He who sees God'.

Ana'el is Governor of the second Heaven, where he is in charge of prayer ascending from the first Heaven. He has a relationship to Earth, from his female side, together with the Archangel Lumi'el (male), one of the angels of creation.

He is mentioned in the Zohar as 'a special ruler', Ana'el (Anahel), who is in charge of many forces who stands at the twelfth entrance, and when the prayer ascends, proclaims to all the entrances: 'Open all ye gates.' (Isaiah 26:2.), that the righteous nation may enter…'

In addition he controls kingdoms and kings on earth, and along with Gabri'el, he has dominion over the moon.

Archangel Ana'el is Chief of Virtues along with Cervi'el, and is in charge of the Order of Principalities, Authorities and the angelic order of the Elohim. Among this order are angels associated with the heavenly Father under the authority of Ana'el, and like him, are sources of inspiration.

The Order of Principalities is the third group in the hierarchy of angels, and their role is to be caretakers over every nation on earth. They are empowered with the great strength of the Creator to have a direct impact on the affairs of humanity, and can, if summoned, move a vast nation of hearts and minds to bring about change for the betterment of our planet.

To anthroposophist along with Jewish lore and angelology, Ana'el is often included in lists as being one of the seven archangels. Saint Gregory names them as, Ana'el, Gabri'el, Mikh'ael, Oriphi'el, Rapha'el, Sama'el and Zakari'el. They are all foreseen to have a unique task to act as a global 'time spirit', each for a period of around 380 years.

In Babylonian times, the ancient priest-astronomers communicated with archangel Ana'el to assist them with their forecasting, healing and spiritual work. Some Judaic texts mention Ana'el taking Enoch to the spirit world where he was transformed into archangel Metatron – Enoch was one of only two humans to be transformed into an archangel, apart from the prophet Elijah who became archangel Sandalphon.

Ana'el is related to the Chaldean Ishtar, ruler of Venus therefore linking with Luc'ifer.

Apart from variations already mentioned, Ana'el is, or appears to be Aniyel, Anaphi'el (Anafi'el), Aufi'el. In *The Tempest* by William Shakespeare, Ana'el is combined with Uri'el to form the sprite Ari'el.

Ari'el was also quoted by Sir Edward Kelley to be a 'conglomerate of Ana'el and Uri'el'. In Longfellow's *The Golden Legend*, Ana'el is one of the angels of the seven planets, specially the angel of the Star of Love, the Evening Star or Venus and Ruler of Friday angels.

Archangel Ana'el is also an Angelic Ambassador of Intuition, supporting those who wish to open and develop their intuitive and psychic power. He reminds us that our abilities are innate and are already part of our consciousness; we *all* have 'psychic' powers, though many of us use our intuition without being knowingly aware. We may just follow our 'gut' feelings or we 'just know' what to do without realizing that this is our natural instinctive consciousness at work within our lives.

Then again, there are many that wish to be more consciously aware of their intuitive and psychic powers in order to use these abilities to further their own individual training and personal life development. Others may wish to channel the energy professionally, but whatever the purpose may be, Archangel

Ana'el is the perfect angelic assistant for further developing our natural intuitive and psychic powers.

Ana'el has the power to be able to turn something that is barren into something fruitful, and change your mood from one of great sadness to happiness. If you feel your life is incomplete, invoke Archangel Ana'el to assist you.

He will often appear, and show you how to fill the gaps in your life with events and things that make life worth living. He symbolizes friendship, beauty, and pleasure and as he exercises dominion over the planet Venus, is one of the luminaries concerned with human sexuality.

Jewish folklore states that as an angel of the principalities he carries a sceptre, cross and sword. On other occasions Ana'el takes the form an extremely beautiful woman. There are many conflicting descriptions of the Archangel Ana'el some believe that the angel is 5'2" tall with straight light blond hair and one pair of large cream wings, others an androgynous figure approximately 6' 0" tall with long black hair and large grey wings. Some also say that the angel appears robed in an emerald green tunic carrying a lantern in one hand, and in the other a wand tipped with a pine cone decorated with multi-coloured ribbons. But in all representations of this angel whether male of female, Ana'el always has a rose symbolising enfoldment, spiritual growth, love and beauty.

Negative aspects: Coldness, isolation and lechery.

Positive: Vision of the Divine Dominion Virtue – Inspiration, artistic talent, and harmony.

Magical Intentions: Venus's energies are warm, sensuous, and fulfilling. Efforts that involve any type of pleasure, comfort, and luxury, as well as the arts and music work well on his day, Friday. As Venus lends its sensuous influences to the energies of this day, use it for any magical work that deals with matters of the heart, romance, marriage, sexual matters, physical beauty, friendship, strangers and partnerships. If your request concerns love, to have any kind of ring given to you – even a curtain ring, or to find a ring in the street this is a sign that Ana'el has granted your request.

Rulership: Ana'el rules all matters of peace, beauty, grace and art and brings harmony and inspiration to our lives. He is a master of the lessons of polarity and duality and of synchronicity. It is this angel who brings together friends and lovers and then supports them in their relationships. He is the angel of love and peace, receiver of prayers, beauty, gentleness, femininity, harmony and imagination. Ana'el is the patron angel of students, teachers and learning. He is the creator of beautiful things. Garden magic, individual income, anything to do with growth invoke this angel.

As with Luc'ifer, Ana'el is generally associated with the planet Venus, he is also the archangel of the Yetzirah Sephirah of Netzach. He rules two signs of the zodiac, Libra ♎ (positive) and Taurus ♉ (negative). Colours representative of him are emerald green and royal blue.

Throughout the pathworking many signs and symbolic forms will be revealed to you and it is important that you remember them, especially if you intend writing letters of petition.

When writing to this angel, first draw his three symbols, write 'To Archangel Ana'el' followed by the letter of request, all of which is written in Passing of Rivers Script and finally sign your secret name.

The letter must be written on a Friday at the appointed hour (see chart), using white paper and blue ink for Taurus, and pink paper and Red ink for Libra. The letter is kept for a lunar month (Twenty-eight days) and on the fourth Friday it is burnt.

Ana'el may use one or several of the signs during the course of the twenty-eight days, but one sign is enough to assume your request has been granted.

If you receive no sign from him, your request is refused. Magical help is not intended to take the place of your own efforts.

Magical letters can be written to any of the Ruling Angels but only on matters He rules, and on His day, you need to invoke or banish.

Do not complicate this system beyond what is given, as the letter is sufficient. Simplicity is the beauty of this art, the Voice of Angels is not a ritual, add the knowledge to what you already have and don't confuse systems.

> 'May the Archangel Ana'el grant
> and bless your request'

Path to Ana'el

What you will need:
Oil of frankincense, incense, charcoal, goblet of wine/beer, fruit juice or water, two green candles, and a statue or picture of the angel (optional but very useful).

Preparation:
Don your white robe and tie an emerald green cord around your waist. This will be in respect for the Angel you will be working with. Anoint wrists, temples and throat with oil of frankincense. Light candles. Prepare charcoal and add incense as required. Fill goblet with liquid and raise it in salutation to the angels and place it back on your altar.

Sit comfortably in an upright chair and inhale very slowly and deeply. You are not just inhaling air, but joy, serenity, strength, vitality, courage, and whichever positive quality you want to affirm. Imagine the breath filling not only your lungs, but also the whole body – starting from the feet and culminating at a point between the eyebrows.

As you exhale not only do you expel carbon dioxide from your system, but also mental and emotional impurities such as weakness, discouragement and despair. Feel the intimate connection between the mind and the breath. Feel the flow of energy around your body as you prepare for your ritual working.

Say the temple prayer to the angels:

I call upon thy sacred name

Of the being that has been with me

Since the beginning of beginnings.

As I gaze upwards

May I behold thy beauty and thy splendour unto eternity,

Time without end.

Build your gate with love and care; visualise Angel Hair quartz crystal the colour of citrine pushing up through the earth, towering above your head and disappearing into the heavens. Visualise a brilliant shaft of light pass through it. Marvel at the smoky golden brown strands tipped with red sparks of colour as spirits dance within. Rising from the ten-edged crystal platform, and obscuring the abyss below, are clouds of sulphur dioxide that are being pushed up into the air by the solar winds that are giving off a high pitched whistling sound. Luc'ifer is nowhere to be found, and the ever-rising clouds are making it difficult for you to see the edge of the platform.

'It is often said that the surface of my planet Venus resembles an inferno!' It is Luc'ifer, and as your guardian takes you by the hand, the wall breaks through the clouds. Five archangels peer out at you; their gaze seems frozen behind the dense crystal cells.

'Come Pilgrim, let us escape these fumes and go to a higher elevation where it's cooler.'

The inner voices ring out: 'All man is Divine' – like a sponge, your heart absorbs the words. The seventh cell wall dissolves as you both pass through it.

'Call forth the Archangel Ana'el, Pilgrim.' Luc'ifer whispers to you.

Pause before beginning your invocation. Visualise each word as you utter it. Breathe it into life; endow it with passion and sincerity. Each is a rhythmic element combining to form a powerful symphony, imbue your call with such beauty that the angelic being cannot but help to respond. Not only will you be invoking Ana'el, but going on a journey into the centre of his realm. You will learn how to focus on his energy as you are drawn in. This is your gateway.

'Divine Prince of the Angels,

Great Angel of Prophetic Vision,

Angel of Glory and Grace,

Through your Glory and Grace is light,

And it is through this light

That one sees the Great Creator.

Defender of the elements, air and earth

Safe keeper of prayers ascending from the First Heaven

Thou who art Ruler of the Second Heaven – Shehaqim.

Ruler of the Eastern and Northern Rivers,

Watcher of the East and North,

Open my heart and my mind

That I may feel you, and know you,

I pray thee, show me a sign

And receive me into your realm'

An unseen hand writes Archangel Ana'el on one of the cell walls.

Ana'el

an-A-EL.

Commit it to memory. This symbol is charged, look at each mark and take it within.

Luc'ifer stands by your side, and together you look through vaporous clouds at the thousands of impact craters evenly distributed over the surface of Venus; their well-preserved condition indicates that the planet underwent a global resurfacing event over five hundred million years ago – unlike the Earth where degradation is caused by wind and rain erosion. Take a deep breath and say:

'Come, Spirits adorned in the glow of Venus,

Radiant Spirits who are ready to obey the power of the ancient tongue,

Come assist me in the operation that I am making.

With the aid of the Majestic light,

O Splendour of Inn-on,

That which the Eternal Creator hath formed,

I invoke thee for these purposes.

I pray thee, be favourable to what I shall ask.

In the Name of the beings who surround and reflect the Mighty Ana'el,

Heavenly angel, guard me.'

The sulphuric gas cloud is replaced by a wash of blue and green light. A green wilderness like forest spreads up to the low mountains; the sun is shining, and your body drinks in its warmth, and your soul drinks in its gold. Your ears are full of warm and drowsy sounds that sharpen to become the bird-song of love birds. Glorious coloured blue tits take flight and then settle on the branches of a large apple tree, heavy with fruit, some of which has fallen to your feet. You watch a fat caterpillar as it lazily crawls onto the juicy fruits. The air is heavy with the perfume of roses that mingles with the delicate scent of tall-stemmed delphiniums that spring up all around you. A butterfly settles on your left arm and a small rabbit scuttles across your feet. Pilgrim, these are the signs and symbols of Ana'el take in all you hear, smell and see, and invoke.

'Hail Ana'el!

I thank thee for these magical signs.

Around me is the exhilarating scent of Musk, Violet, Sandalwood and Mint,

May each inhalation that fills my lungs

Intensify my awareness of thee,

Hail be to Ana'el!'

Pause to allow your conscious mind to take in events so far, let it become like a mirror, reflecting, but allowing light of the skies above bathe you and sanctify you.

Conjuration

'I ….. (utter your secret name) salute thee and conjure thee,

Through the love of Venus,

O most beautiful Luminary,

By the heavy air that surrounds me,

By the strange gases above me,

By the names of the spirit princes living in you,

By the ineffable name by which created everything!

By the planet name of NVGH.

By you, O resplendent One, appear!

Ruler of the Second Heaven Shehaqim

I conjure thee.

Grace my eyes with your presence

Archangel Ana'el, appear before me!'

From above delicate pink rose petals fall about your feet. Drink in the aroma Pilgrim, and say:

Bless-ed be He,

Bless-ed be the Archangel

Bless-ed be He

Hail Great One! Hail Ana'el!

Hal Al Ha Na Ana'el

Thou who now stands before me

Thou who's image is that of a most beautiful androgynous being

Thou who's face shines with golden light

Copper is the colour of your hair.

Of deepest green are your eyes,

Brilliant light radiates from your heart

Sparkling with all the colours of a diamond

Your mouth is soft as flower petals

O that they may speak words so precious

That only my ears alone will hear your voice.

Your angelic words are but the echo of the Creator,

Like music of pure and untouched revelation.

Elegant is your fine form robed in translucent emerald-green

Magical is the seven-pointed star that hangs from your delicate neck

The movement of your transparent wings are barely perceived in vision,

In your right hand, you hold a wand tipped with a pinecone decorated with multi-coloured ribbons.

In your right hand you carry a lantern,

The light of which forms the talisman above your head

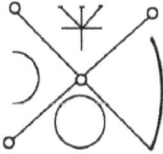

May I understand its meaning and take it within my heart.

I, the Pilgrim stand before you enthralled,

May the beauty of your spirit rest within my soul.'

Cloud wreaths of rose-red surround you. Wings, delicate and airy as the gossamers of a dragonfly touch you; it is the planetary spirit and ethereal soul of Venus, Kedemel. His pale pink eyes look upon you tenderly, Pilgrim. Within this look is his sigil , take it within.

Wave upon wave of light washes over you and emerging from the glow is Venus' planetary intelligence, Hagi'el proudly displaying his sigil . He is closely followed by Venus' planetary spirit Hagit who holds a shield of copper, and on it, is embossed his sigil . As he floats around you he whispers in your ear:

'I am able to make all people who gaze upon me beautiful, and I turn copper into gold and gold into copper.'

In the Western region of the ocean of the sky the golden orb of the sun floats behind the highest mountain bathing the rim in red-orange tides. The afterglow is like an exquisite spasm, a beautiful, almost desperate effort ending in the quiet darkness of defeat.

Ana'el raises the lantern in his right hand, and pointing his wand at the ground tiny glittering lights appear, silver-white like diamonds. As you bend down to touch them, squashy little bodies make you recoil; these are the thousand glow-worms that have come to light the double-sided Kamea.

22	47	16	41	10	35	4
5	23	48	17	42	11	29
30	6	24	49	18	36	12
13	31	7	25	43	19	37
38	14	32	1	26	44	20
21	39	8	33	2	27	45
46	15	40	9	34	3	28

Each mark and number emits tones that impact upon you, a voice says:

'Within this square are divine names, Pilgrim, of the Intelligence, Spirit and Intelligences – sacred to Ana'el through Venus.'

Through this strange twilight Archangel Ana'el smiles, and raising his lantern once again, colour returns to the sky – ethereal colour, wavering as if it ought not to return. You look around; the light looks strangely purified, and full of crystal coldness. The birds that flew against it are no longer birds, but dark, moving ornaments.

Apples, black cherries, a coconut, gooseberries, figs, strawberries and tomatoes fall from the sky and land in a delicious jumble on to a copper platter that has landed at your feet.

Next to the platter is a burning brazier and dish filled with Saffron, Verbena, Sandalwood and Myrtle. Instinct tells you to make an offering. Say:

'I pray thee Archangel Ana'el

Bringer of love and gracious angel of Venus

Receive these perfumed fumigations

May the rising flames from these herbs

Ignite my courage and send it into your realm.

I bow to thee Ana'el,

Chief of the Order of Principalities and Virtues

I open my heart to you

And rejoice in your presence.'

In the mystery of the moment, in the mystery of the silence that softly showers out of the aromas, Luc'ifer appears, holding the sacred ring of Solomon and crimson red silk tabard. Take the ring Pilgrim, put it on the index finger of your right hand, put the tabard over your shoulders, feel the power from these sacred objects rise within you, and say:

'I receive the ring and tabard,

May that I wear these with pride.'

It is at this stage where you may want to take some personal time with Ana'el for quiet introspection, conversation, meditation or whatever you need to build and cultivate your relationship with the archangel. Say:

'I feel the power from these sacred objects rise within me,

I feel my minds eye open

Thus I am ready O Great and Divine Being,

Great Archangel Ana'el I pray thee,

Open my eyes so that I may see the sacred.'

Luc'ifer looks at his brother and nods his head. Ana'el raises his pine tipped wand in the air, the ribbons float in ethereal colours in a breeze of their own. Within this breeze, a great swarm of bees hum and move slowly in the golden air. They leisurely pass you and settle on a space in front of Luc'ifer and Ana'el. Drowsily the bees work, and presently, moved by some prompting instinct they rise in one single body and fly off leaving behind them soft wax.

Together with the might of their sacred breath, the two archangel's burn letters and numbers into the wax form, and say:

'Zamran micalzo od ozazm urelp,
Lap zir Ioiad.'

'Show yourselves in power and make me a strong seething.
For, I am of Him that liveth forever.'

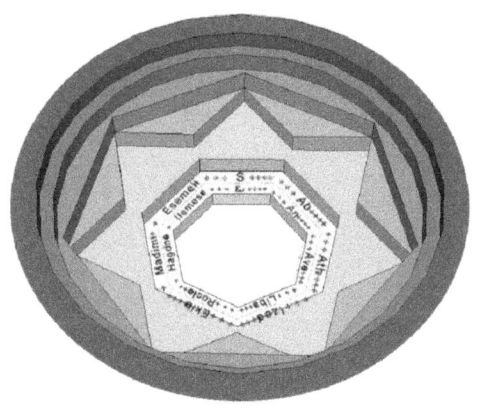

'Behold the Seal of Truth is again revealed. Pilgrim, take in all you see, walk upon the seal and feel the mystery within.'

As you descend the steps multiple sounds ring out and within the sounds letters and numbers intensify and fade as you pass from level to level. Star-forms followed by double heptagons emerge, and impact on your visual senses. But within the epicentre is the Abyss intense, extreme with an unforgiving environment and the endless existential void of infinite space. Divine shapes appear and disappear leaving behind them a hallowed light.

There follows a silence, Luc'ifer and Ana'el look down at you as you struggle to find the words – you *will* find the words Pilgrim! Take a deep breath, and through the deafening silence, say:

"Great Archangel of Venus,

Thou art most splendid in thy magic,

I behold the mystery within.

Hail, the Sons of Light!

Hail, the Daughters of Light!'

The light forms dim and brighten as you recognize their presence.

'May every Daughter of Light bringeth forth a Daughter.

Hail the Daughters of Daughters which is 7!

'May every Son of Light bringeth forth a Son

Hail, The Sons of the Sons which is 7!'

An unimaginable spectrum of colours dance before your eyes, colours that light every rim, heptagon and angle of the seal. A stream of happiness flows in and through you carrying the message of joy, divine joy that is the sole purpose of life.

With the same mite as their sacred breath that created the letters and numbers on the seal, Luc'ifer and Ana'el slowly melt the wax beneath your feet, leaving a grey cratered surface of Venus behind.

It is now time for you to leave the angelic realm of Ana'el.

Stand silently, and think about what you have uttered, what has been said to you and foremost, what has been revealed. Ask yourself Pilgrim: Has this experience changed me? Close your eyes and when you open them say these words:

'Eternal are the Archangels and Angels whose celestial realms endureth, forever and ever. I return thanks unto the Great Creator, in Whose Name thou, Ana'el hast come. Depart hence in peace unto thine habitations, and be thou ready to return when so ever I shall have need of thee.'

Utter your secret name to the angels, go through the portal into your world and seal the door behind you.

>'May the Archangel Ana'el guard
>and bless you and keep you safe'

8
Archangel Cassi'el
'Speed of God'

Legend

The name Cassi'el is Latin in origin. He is also known by Casi'el, Kafzi'el, Qaspi'el, Quaphsi'el and Qafsi'el. He is regarded as the Angel of Peace and Harmony whose symbol is the Dove. Within post-biblical Judeo-Christian religion Cassi'el is a holy archangel, particularly that of the Kabbalah. In the Zoah, along with Hizki'el, Cassi'el served as one of Gabri'el's chief followers during the angelic battles.

What is unusual about Cassi'el within scripture as mainstream Judaism and Christianity are concerned, he is not associated with any specific tasks or angel-like qualities. One could say that Cassi'el is unlike many of the other archangels; he is simply known as a watcher, bearing witness to all the events that unfold within our universe, or in the Creator's making. It is said that Cassi'el is forbidden to intervene with any of the events that he is witnessing develop. What is even stranger is that scripture goes on to state: 'he is the angel of solitude and tears who shews forth the unity of the eternal kingdom'.

As angel of tears and temperance Cassi'el is known to preside over the death or passing of any great ruler or king. In this sense, he is rather a melancholy angel, differing greatly from his archangel brothers.

Cassi'el is patron angel of the oppressed, the downtrodden, the impoverished, the enslaved, orphaned children and the unjustly persecuted.

Occultists, from very early times figured Cassi'el prominently in their writings claiming him to be the Sarim or Prince Regent of the choir of angels called the Powers and the Regent and guardian of the Halls of the Seventh Heaven. He is also included in lists as being one of the seven Gnostic archangels who rules Saturn.

Cassi'el is said to be the angel to invoke with a charm to drive away enemies; in ancient times the words were written on parchment with the blood of a bird, and then tied to the foot of a dove. If the dove flew away, it took the enemy with it. If the dove refused to fly, it was a sign that enemies would not depart.

Although Cassi'el to our knowledge has not been depicted in any paintings, in *The Picture Museum of Sorcery, Magic and Alchemy* by Emile Grillot de Gilvry, is a reproduction of a page out of the 'Book of Spirits' showing how to conjure Cassi'el. In this book and also *The Magus* or *Celestial Intelligencer*, a handbook of the occult and ceremonial magic compiled by Francis Barrett, is Cassi'el's sigil and signature. In *The Magus*, he is called Cassi'el Mocoton and pictures him as a bearded jinni, riding a dragon. In the second book of *The Magus*, Cassi'el and Mocoton are two separate entities.

This angel's greatest gifts are tolerance, patience and strengthening of inner convictions; giving the strength to work and to have inner discipline and belief in ourselves. He is also said to be the bringer of the Red Healing Light, within it carrying energy and passion. He holds the power to help you bring works into being and create quickly.

In life there is always a paradox, it is the archangel Cassi'el who brings balance; light – dark, joy – sorrow, excitement – anxiety, you cannot appreciate one without the other, and as the two go together, we need to be able to experience them together. We would not know when we were happy if we were never sad.

Cassi'el usually arrives in your life when you are at your darkest hour, feeling abandoned by all that you hold dear. When your heart is heaviest and overflowing with tears, Cassi'el appears to help shoulder the burdens of your woes and keep feelings of hopelessness at bay. He brings you comfort and reminds you of the good times past, and shows the way to good times to come.

From our tears comes our ultimate pleasure. The emotions in the body are very similar; it is how we decide to experience them that make them different. A new job for example can be both exciting and daunting; Cassi'el helps you to keep things in perspective.

We are all one with the Creator and can tap in to the 'collective unconscious' (as Carl Jung calls it) or connect to the cosmic web so you can send and receive love and light at all times therefore bringing more love and healing to the world. Being in harmony with yourself and your life means taking time to 'be' rather than 'do'; to find your inner centre and become one with yourself and your life.

Cassi'el's message to the contemporary world could be: 'for with what judgment ye judge, ye shall be judged: and with what measure ye mete, it shall be measured to you again.' (Matthew 7:2)

Accessing the Source is Archangel Cassi'el's specialty. He is a manifestor born out of the understanding of desire; 'de Sire' meaning, 'of God'. This angel holds the power to create new realities quickly, and is naturally drawn to divine frequencies. He presides over dolphins, and other oceanic life. Water is a divine conductor and Cassi'el gathers its energy by using it to cleanse away feelings of negativity, leaving clarity on hand to heal, feel and reveal. Cassi'el will draw you into places of worship; places where the divine is strongly present, on sacred grounds and in the sanctity of your own prayer circle. All Cassi'el asks of you is to give thanks for all your blessings and in return he will bestow upon you the power to share your spiritual gifts with others.

In health he may be petitioned on all matters to do with the left leg. Complaints that are the natural results of old age, these may not cure but he will relieve them, among them rheumatism, cramps, and all ills caused by cold or damp.

Here are some of the things the Angel Cassi'el will help you with:

Magical Intentions: Home, houses, land and property, all old people, poverty, astral knowledge, esoteric knowledge farming and examinations. Saturn is the planet of karma; His day is an excellent time for spell work involving reincarnation, karmic lessons, the mysteries, wisdom, and long-term projects. It is also a good time to begin work that deals with the elderly and disease. Spirit communications, meditation, psychic attack or defence, locating lost things and missing persons, life, doctrine, protection, knowledge, authority, limitations, boundaries, time and death.

Rulerships: The Angel Cassi'el has rulership over legacies, and settlements of will or affairs of the deceased. He manages all matters of housing, property, and repairs of property. He also aids the retired. He brings stability into life and helps in all matters that take time to work. He governs business, politics, agriculture, mining, archaeology, banks, debts, discipline, history, institutions, karmic debts, limitations, longevity, magical knowledge, sacred wisdom, time, morality, and responsibility, protection from poisoning or conspiracy. He is the Angel of mind expansion, memory and genius, and the astral plane.

Negative aspects: Oppression, pain.

The Archangels Cassi'el and Uri'el are a class of Teaching Angels known also as the 'Angels of Men' and will help students who have other Astrological signs different from those of Aquarius and Capricorn.

The Angel Cassi'el rules one sign of the zodiac only, that of Capricorn ♑, the sign of the goat, symbolized by a letter 'V' with a hook on one side, the hieroglyph for the beard of the goat. Colours representative of him are black and brown.

When writing to this angel, draw his four symbols, write 'To Archangel Cassi'el' and the request in Malachim and finally sign your secret name in Passing the Rivers Script.

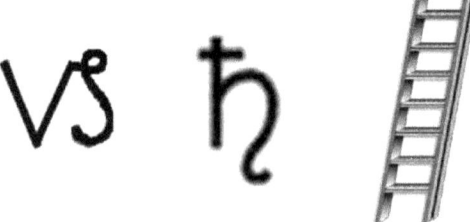

The letter to this angel must be written on white paper, using either black ink or lead pencil (lead being Saturn's metal). This angel does not work quickly, but slowly and surely, so patience is needed in waiting for his signs. It is to be written on a Saturday at the appointed hour (see chart) kept for seven days, and burnt on the following Saturday. The day of writing counts as one day.

Cassi'el speaks very slowly and is a very powerful teaching angel. He is sometimes known as the angel of temperance and if he appears as a guardian angel, you may have many lessons to learn in your life regarding patience and moderation.

Cassi'el may use one or several of the signs during the course of the seven days, but one sign is enough to assume your request has been granted. If you receive no sign from Cassi'el, your request is refused. Do not repeat your letters until seven days have elapsed. Signs will not be given to you until the time is right. Magical help is not intended to take the place of your own efforts.

Magical letters can be written to any of the Ruling Angels but only on matters He rules, and on His day, you need to invoke or banish.

Do not complicate this system beyond what is given, as the letter is sufficient. Simplicity is the beauty of this art; the Voice of Angels is not a ritual system, just add the knowledge to what you already have.

'May the Archangel Cassi'el grant
and bless your request'

Path to Cassi'el

What you will need:
Oil of frankincense, incense, charcoal, goblet of wine/beer, fruit juice or water, two black candles, a statue or picture of the angel (optional but very useful).

Preparation:
Don your white robe and tie a black or brown cord around your waist. This will be in respect for the Angel you will be working with. Anoint wrists, temples and throat with oil of frankincense. Light candles. Prepare charcoal and add incense as required. Fill goblet with liquid and raise it in salutation to the angels and place it back on your altar.

Sit comfortably in an upright chair and inhale very slowly and deeply. You are not just inhaling air, but joy, serenity, strength, vitality, courage, and whichever positive quality you want to affirm. Imagine the breath filling not only your lungs, but also the whole body – starting from the feet and culminating at a point between the eyebrows.

As you exhale not only do you expel carbon dioxide from your system, but also mental and emotional impurities such as weakness, discouragement and despair. Feel the intimate connection between the mind and the breath. Feel the flow of energy around your body as you prepare for your ritual working.

Say the temple prayer to the angels:

I call upon thy sacred name

Of the being that has been with me

Since the beginning of beginnings.

As I gaze upwards

May I behold thy beauty and thy splendour unto eternity,

Time without end.

Build your gate with love and care; visualise Angel Hair quartz crystal the colour of citrine pushing up through the earth, towering above your head and disappearing into the heavens. Visualise a brilliant shaft of light pass through it. Marvel at the smoky golden brown strands tipped with red sparks of colour as spirits dance within.

Cold and dry is this planet Saturn. An overwhelming feeling of distress, failure and dejection hits you. A wave of sorrow encompasses you. O that I may escape this miserable place, you cry. O that I may leap into the yawning abyss below that is more welcoming than Saturn! As you begin to free-fall your guardian Luc'ifer suddenly pulls you back to the platform.

His smile is warm; he raises his gentle hands, and says: 'Pilgrim, may your negative fears be replaced by fame, success, honour, justice, love, wisdom, leadership ability, authority and long life.'

He raises his left hand, splitting the air, bringing forth ten crystal walls that erupt from the abyss and tower above. Inner voices ring out: 'All man is Divine' – feel the words within your heart.

As Luc'ifer's fingers touch the surface a tumultuous blast of horns rip through the atmosphere cascading crystal shards away; each piece is a rhythmic element that combines to form a powerful symphony. This eighth cell wall dissolves for you both to pass through it.

 'Call forth the Archangel Cassi'el, Pilgrim.' Luc'ifer tells you.

Pause before beginning your invocation. Visualise each word as you utter it. Breathe it into life; endow it with passion and sincerity. Each is a rhythmic element combining to form a powerful symphony, imbue your call with such beauty that the angelic being cannot but help to respond. Not only will you be invoking Cassi'el, but going on a journey into the centre of his realm. You will learn how to focus on his energy as you are drawn in. This is your gateway.

'Great Teaching Angel – Araboth

Guardian Angel of Planet Aralim

Guardian of the threshold

Between this world and the next.

O Father of Time

By thy sacred name ShBThAI

Receive me into your kingdom.

Open my heart and my mind

That I may feel you and know you.

Thou who art Ruler of the Seventh Heaven

Ruler of the Northern River

Divine One, hear my words,

I pray thee, show me a sign.'

An unseen hand writes Archangel Cassi'el on one of the cell walls.

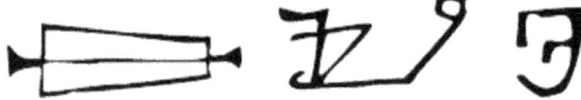

Cassi'el

cas- A-EL

Commit it to memory, this symbol is charged, look at each mark and take it within.

Directly above your head ammonia clouds and gaseous hydrogen sulphide are whipped around by Saturn's winds; the Solar Systems fastest. Further out into space the nine dense ice-particle rings spin around the planet in complex orbital motions of their own. They glint and sparkle like diamonds, and within them revolve the many moonlets, dwarfed against the monster moon Titan, and Enceladus forever emitting jets of gas and dust.

'It is the north polar vortex Pilgrim.' Luc'ifer points out.

Everything appears a bright greenish-blue haze on the northern hemisphere of this planet, but curiously, the light passing through it sheds a golden glow upon a viscous liquid that forms in a continuous hexagonal wave pattern, with each step you take. It is a natural star gate opening before you to pass through.

'Come Spirits that exist in the gaseous realm of Saturn,

Radiant Spirits who are ready to obey the power of the ancient tongue,

Come assist me in the operation that I am making,

With the aid of the Majestic light.

O Splendour of Gala-as,

That which the Eternal Creator hath formed,

I invoke thee for these purposes.

I pray thee, be favourable to what I shall ask.

In the Name of the beings who surround and reflect the Mighty Cassi'el,

Heavenly angel, guard me.'

The landscape around you slowly changes from a pale gold to a variety of greens; trees of Alder, Beech, Cyprus, Oak and Yew appear, followed by variegated ferns that push their way little by little out of the ground; thyme, ivy, evergreen Veronica and Holly.

Fragrant clusters of the showy white Chincherinchee bit by bit sprout, just in time to give a tasty meal to a squirm of worms that lazily crawl up the tender stems.

A brightly coloured parrot takes flight from the foliage alerting you not to step on a tortoise that is in no hurry to move out of your way; its high domed shiny brown shell contrasts with its grey scaly legs.

You bend down and pick up a chunk of coal that litters the ground like black gold.

Pause to allow your conscious mind to take in proceedings so far, let it become like a river flowing always towards enlightenment.

Conjuration

I ... (utter your secret name) salute thee and conjure thee,

O beautiful Saturn!

O wondrous Planet!

By the air that I breathe within me,

By the token of coal I hold: I conjure thee,

By the names of the spirit princes living in you,

By the ineffable name on which created everything!

By you, O resplendent One, appear!

Grace my eyes with your presence.

Archangel Cassi'el, appear before me!

A delicious smell of mimosa pervades the air briefly, only to be swamped by myrrh and patchouli. You are intoxicated by the heady aroma, breathe deeply Pilgrim, and say:

Bless-ed be He,

Bless-ed be the Archangel

Bless-ed be He

Hail Great One! Hail Cassi'el!

Thou who now stands before me

White is your hair that frames an ancient face.

Distant are your grey eyes.

Lamp black is your fine silk robe.

In your right hand is the hourglass of time,

And in your left hand a lantern that will light our way through life.

I see that the flame burns bright, and within I see a strange form

That is cast on the ground before me

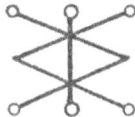

I pray that in time I shall know its meaning.'

With your last utterance Saturn's winds return bringing with it a multitude of airstreams emitting a complex radio spectrum of sounds resulting in auroras that cover both the northern and southern poles with a blanket of colour. First in the aurora is a wave of emerald green, behind it is pink, then a mixture of light green and pale red, followed by pure red, yellow and lastly pure blue. The sounds become more intense, exciting the colours making them more vibrant.

Within this cacophony is the scream of the ethereal Demon Zazel who transmits his sigil in a brief flash of lightning, leaving his mark in tiny flames on the ground in front of you . Cassi'el raises his lantern; the flame within dances and flickers signalling the arrival of his spirit Agi'el , his fabulous colours not only do they ignite the air around you, but send shock waves of sound out into the cosmos. The archangel smiles and nods his head with pleasure. Luc'ifer steps towards him and takes Cassi'el's lantern, and in a grand gesture the archangel raises his left hand and brings down streams of grey light pinpointing it to the ground where it disperses forming a three-sided lead table laden with dried fruits, pomegranates, tomatoes and bitter herbs. Around the edge of the table hang wreaths of deadly nightshade, blue-capped wolfs bane, belladonna flowers, all twined together with lacy strings of hemp. In the air above the table is suspended a glass crucible of burning coals. Luc'ifer steps forward and hands you a pot of black poppy seeds, seedpods of pepperwort, scammony and myrrh. You sprinkle the contents onto the coals, and say:

'I pray thee Archangel Cassi'el

Protector and merciful angel of Saturn,

Receive these perfumed fumigations

May the rising flames from these herbs

Ignite my courage and send it into your realm.

I bow to thee Cassi'el who is ever-waiting and ever-present,

Protector of the entrance between this planet and the next,

I open my heart to you

And rejoice in your presence.'

The black poppy seeds, seedpods of pepperwort and scammony explode when they make contact with the heat of the coals turning the resinous myrrh to a double-sided Kamea.

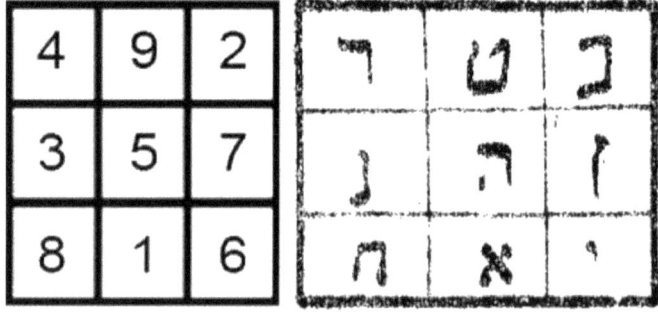

Archangel Cassi'el joyously says:

'Within this square are my divine names, Pilgrim, of my beloved demon Zazel and my spirit Agi'el, sacred to me through Saturn.'

A screeching crow flies in from nowhere dropping the sacred ring of Solomon from its mouth, catch it and put it on the index finger of your right hand. Moving slowly through the ferns, with a steady easy gait, lopes a crocodile. Draped over its huge form is a crimson red silk tabard. The beast pauses in front of Cassi'el, who bends forward and takes the tabard from its back, the crocodile vanishes.

Pilgrim, feel the power and energy as the archangel hangs the tabard over your shoulders. Listen to voice of Cassi'el.

'Ol gnonp prge aldi, od urbs oboleh grasm. Casarm ohorela caba Pir.'

'I garnished with the fire of gathering, and beautified your garments with admiration. To whom I made a law to govern the Holy Ones.'

It is at this stage where you may want to take some personal time with Cassi'el for quiet introspection, conversation, meditation or whatever you need to build and cultivate your relationship with the archangel. Say:

'I pray thee Cassi'el help balance the light and dark within me,
Assist me as I let go all disharmony,
Cassi'el show me how to bring harmony into my life.

As I consciously balance within serenity

I pray that it is reflected in my paths of my life.

Great Archangel Gabri'el I pray thee,

Open my eyes so that I may see the sacred.'

Archangel Cassi'el and Luc'ifer both raise their hands, and so doing, bring in a delicate mist that slowly turns to a shower of gently falling wax. Step by perfect step, by perfect heptagon and interlacing forms arrive at the final stage; the pentagram. Your head held high, you walk down towards the centre of the Seal of Truth, to a tumultuous blast of trumpets.

A voice rings out:

'Truth encompasses everything! ALEPH – TAV – from BEGINNING to END – from BIRTH to DEATH. This is not your death Pilgrim, but your spiritual awakening!'

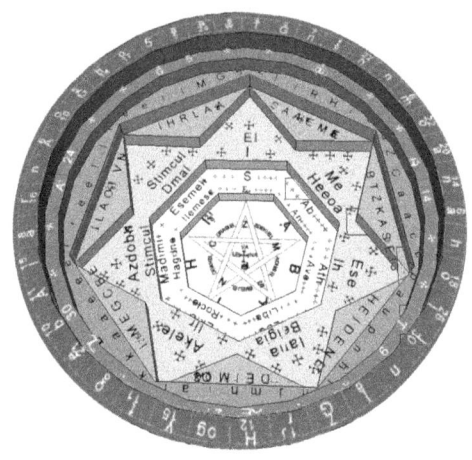

Seven angels stand before the presence of the Great Creator. The Seven planetary archangels place themselves inside the innermost heptagon. The angel of Saturn, Sabathi'el, surrounds the angels of Jupiter- Zadki'el, Mars - Sama'el, Sol - Mikh'ael, Venus - Ana'el and Mercury – Rapha'el; all five are within the angles of the pentagram. The angel of Luna, Levana'el, is wholly inside the central pentagon, surrounding the cross of the Earth.

Say: 'I am encircled in a golden moment,

     A golden miracle that I shall remember until eternity,

     Ye I receive the splendid gift of life

And behold the angels about me.

I walk on through the pentagram and see the great cross of Earth

I see it, and may I live by it.'

Shining with angelic brightness, Luc'ifer steps forward and taking your hands in his, looks deep into your eyes. This moment is frozen in time; it is a wondrous moment for you. The warmth of his voice touches your soul.

'Pilgrim, you have travelled far throughout our angelic realm, and it has been a very testing time for you,' he pauses, 'Your mind is likened to our realm, and many Pilgrims have faced their limits and have visited only a few dominions, leaving the rest in total darkness. In those they chose to visit only a few portals were ever opened.' Luc'ifer draws in his breath and continues, 'You have been to all our dominions, in your mind and in your heart and in doing so the experience has awakened your senses. When you broke the chains that bound me, you also broke the chains that bound your mind. To know and embrace our realm is to know and embrace your self.'

You stand and face the centre of the pentagram, extending your arms to form a cross, concentrate on the feeling of the Creator's energy flowing through you. Close you eyes, and when you open them the angel Rapha'el is before you, his yellow robe floats in the air around you. Behind you there is movement as Gabri'el takes his position, his blue robe makes rippling watery sounds. To your right is Mikh'ael dressed in red, brandishing a sword of pure living flame. On your left is Uri'el, clothed in robes of russet brown, in his right hand he holds a sheaf of golden wheat. The nearness of him gives you the sensation of the element of earth.

Divine light swirls around you, an inner voice says:

'Through the Creator we know how to harness light so exquisitely that only greatness transpires from the vision to the physical, and the substance of the Creators glory and grace is light, and it is through this light that one sees Him.'

It is now time for you to leave the angelic realm of Cassi'el. Stand silently, and think about what you have uttered, what has been said to you and foremost, what has been revealed. Ask yourself Pilgrim: Has this experience changed me? Close your eyes and when you open them say these words:

'Eternal are the Archangels and Angels whose celestial realms endureth, forever and ever. I return thanks unto the Great Creator, in Whose Name thou, Cassi'el hast come. Depart hence in peace unto thine habitations, and be thou ready to return when so ever I shall have need of thee.'

Utter your secret name to the angels, go through the portal into your world and seal the door behind you.

> 'May the Archangels guard and bless you
> and keep you safe'

9
Archangel Uri'el
'Flame of God'

Legend

The name Uri'el literally means 'Flame of God', 'Fire of God', 'El/God is my Light' and even, 'Sun of God'.

Uri'el is one of the four major archangels within traditional Judeo-Christian scripture. The angel's name in Hebrew can be translated to mean 'My Light is God' or 'Light of God'. What has been the source of a lot of debate within some theological academic groups maintain the actual name begins with a 'U', whilst other scholars claim that it is actually the ancient Hebrew 'aleph' an 'A' as in Ari'el. Regardless of the spelling variation, whether it is Uri'el or Ari'el, they are obviously discussing or addressing the same heavenly being

The archangel Uri'el appeared in a vision to Esdras in the second book of Esdras in the Apocrypha, 4:1, 'and the angel that was sent unto me, whose name was Uri'el'. Saint Ambrose, the bishop of Milan, addresses the Archangel Uri'el with the customary 'U', whilst in other ancient and now non canonical law the angel is addressed as Ari'el.

He is one of the angels of vengeance often sent out by the Creator to administer divine justice. Uri'el is the 'Light which shineth in darkness, yet the darkness comprehendeth it not.'

Uri'el is also known as Angel of Sanctification, Angel of Glory, Angel of Face and Angel of Presence. The title Angel of Presence is often taken to mean Shekinah, used to signify the dwelling or settling in the presence of the Creator.

As stated in *Midrash Rabbah* (Num. 2:10), Uri'el is one of the four angels whom the Creator placed around His throne. These four angels radiate their light on the four winds of heaven, but the light that radiates over the Earth, the most perfect, is that of Uri'el.

In the Kabbalah, including the Zohar, these angels of the Presence are identified with the four holy beasts that Ezeki'el saw in the Merkabah and the figure of Uri'el with that of the eagle, and sometimes with that of the lion.

The Zohar (I, 6b; III, 32b, 211a) attributes Uri'el a special purpose in connection with the sacrifices at the time of the First Temple. The altar, which is called Ari'el (Isa. 29:1–2), is named after Uri'el, who descended in the likeness of a lion to crouch on the altar and devoured the sacrifices. This brought joy to the priest and the children of Israel as they saw it as a sign that the offerings had been accepted with favour.

Trying to define Uri'el is not an easy undertaking as he appears to be a composite of numerous names and countless qualities, and those that are documented in this text reveal similarities that may link the confusing sources and traditions.

Some of this confusion could have been as a result of Uri'el being condemned to Hell by the Council of Rome in 745 CE. Such a powerful archangel would undoubtedly have continued to be held in great regard by the populace and by adopting other aliases Uri'el would avoid confrontation with the Church. Whether he is a composite of all the angelic names listed or other angels have been incorrectly included is always questionable and open to discussion. Whatever name we call him, he remains a harsh and punishing angel of vengeance and said to be chief of the seven Archangels. One of Uri'el's responsibilities is delivering punishment to those condemned to Tartarus or Hell.

Pope St Zachary in a move to simplify the Church's teaching of angels, condemned the obsession of worshipping them as angelolatry, but sanctioned the practice of the reverence angels such as; Mikh'ael, Gabri'el and Rapha'el mentioned in the recognized Catholic canon of scriptures. It was agreed by the synod of the Council of Rome to remove particular angels, and that unfortunately included Uri'el.

This angel is often referred to as the Great Archangel of the Earth. Today he could be seen as keeper of the mysteries that are at hidden depths of the living world. Uri'el is said to be the protector against terror, thunder, lightning, earthquakes, cataclysms, and volcanic eruptions.

His heavenly or spiritual role is principally the angel who guides the deceased during the Last Judgement, drawing another connection between the angel and the 'Raging Fire of God's Judgement', and as mentioned above, Uri'el's name also means 'The Light of God'.

Another of his heavenly duties is thought to be responsible for, is watcher of the South. Whereas most other archangels primarily fulfil duties in heaven, Uri'el is the angel with very deep ties to the Earth and humanity.

The *Book of the Watchers* (2nd century BCE) is the second oldest book in the Enochic corpus, tells us that Uri'el, Rapha'el and Gabri'el were present before the Creator to testify on behalf of humankind. These angels asked for divine intervention during the reign of the Grigori, Fallen Watchers as they had taken human wives who went on to produce half angel, half human offspring called, Nephilim. Uri'el was responsible for contacting Noah about the impending Great Flood. For the remainder of the Book of the Watchers, and in many of the other books that make up 1 Enoch, Uri'el acts as a guide for Enoch.

In art, Uri'el is featured in the two versions of Virgin on the Rocks, a painting by Leonardo da Vinci, where the angel is seen to the right of Mary, Elizabeth and the infant John. Other pictures were produced spanning several centuries in three continents including stained glass windows.

In the early 12th century Renaissance period Pope Clement III reportedly ordered the removal of Uri'el's image from the church of Santa Maria del Angeli in Rome, and further instructions were given for a painting of the angel Uri'el in the church in Piazza Esedra to be painted over. The reason seems to have been a misguided concept that Uri'el was in some way associated with the Johannine heresy that claimed John the Baptist was the true Messiah, and not his cousin Jesus, however no evidence was found to prove such a connection. The unjust criticism heaped upon Uri'el by the Church of Rome was ignored by the Spanish and Portuguese-speaking countries, and in South America there can still be found the most worship for this archangel. There are also many centres of devotion to be found in the Church of England and the Episcopal Church in the United States.

According to the 16th century scholar, Dr Johannes Dee's diary notes, May 25, 1581, he first saw spirits while crystal gazing. During the following year, he saw an apparition of the angel Uri'el, who gave him a convex piece of crystal that would enable him to communicate with the spirit world. Dr Dee's scrying assistant, Edward Kelly saw an angel in a crystal ball who Dee identified the being, from his Kabbalistic knowledge as 'Uri'el, the angel of light.'

Whether this angel is depicted in religion, magical scrying, paintings, stained glass, or in the poem *Paradise Lost* by John Milton, this archangel continues to command the imagination, reverence, and devotion of people around the world.

His influence is believed to peak during the summer months when the feast day of the Archangel Uri'el is celebrated July 28. According to Corinne Heline, an American author, Christian mystic and occultist born in Atlanta, Georgia, 1882 –1975): 'The beautiful Uri'el stands guardian over the activities of the summer. The ripening of grain and the floodtide of blossom are under his guidance. He also supervises the Nature Spirits, those fascinating little sprites who inhabit the elements of earth, air, fire and water, and who lend so much to the beautification of all nature. The highest initiatory teachings belonging to the New Age... are under the direction of Uri'el.' *The Blessed Virgin Mary.* New Age Press, 1971, p. 110.

Archangel Uri'el appears as a young man with black hair bearing grey streaks. He wears a bodice of dark blue with a cloak of the same colour he carries in his right hand a crystal tipped wand. It is also said that between his brows glows the astrological of Uranus. As an angel, Uri'el is seen with a scroll and a book.

Magical Intentions: Primarily He is the angel of magical force, and his main work is to help magic practice work, enabling you to be led into and out of initiations, and to bring about changes in your life towards the development of your soul to spirit. Therefore ask him only on these matters. If he is evoked to cause and effect, or to banish something, be prepared for it to come in a sudden or devastating way, this is shown in his sign … the lightning flash.

Rulerships: Magic of tumultuous change, revolution, the unexpected and the force of magnetism. All inspiration, astrology and issues of divorce. He deals with matters of eccentricity, the avant-garde, and craziness. Therefore petition Uri'el for all nervous complaints, for he has rulership of the nervous system. As a saint, Uri'el has the symbol of an open hand bearing a flame. This angel teaches the path of the heart, and the fire of pure Love. Without this pure Love and devotion to Spirit, all spiritual and mystical study would remain a mere intellectual pursuit, fairy gold. This understanding of true spiritual study is further supported by the tradition that Uri'el brought to Earth: Alchemy, the heavenly arcane, he is also credited with giving the gift of Kabbalah to humankind. Uri'el is instrumental in the lesser banishing ritual of the pentagram, the invocation includes the words: 'Before me Rapha'el; behind me Gabri'el; on my right hand Mikh'ael; on my left hand Auri'el (Uri'el) …

Negative aspects: revolution

The Angel Uri'el rules one sign of the zodiac only, that of Aquarius ♒. Colours representative of him are deep blue and green.

When writing to this angel, first draw his three symbols, write 'To Uri'el Angel and Magical Force', using Celestial Script throughout the address, followed by the letter of request, all of which is written in Theban Script and finally sign your secret name in Passing of Rivers Script. Do not ask the Archangel Uri'el to help in a matter you can perform yourself for a Throne Angel may help and assist you but he is not a servant of mankind.

The letter to this angel must be written on white paper with green ink. It is to be written on a Saturday at the appointed hour (see chart) and kept for fourteen days. The day of writing counts as one day, and on the fourteenth day, the letter is burnt.

The Archangel Uri'el should never be invoked lightly, unless he is one of your ruling angels. He can and does perform miracles and his ways are swift, so never petition Uri'el unless you are prepared for sudden upheavals and unexpected happenings, for he is a Throne Angel with overwhelming power, and the force of magic itself.

Uri'el may use one or several of the signs during the course of the fourteen days, but one sign is enough to assume your request has been granted. If you receive no sign from him, your request is refused. Do not repeat your letters until seven days have elapsed. Signs will not be given to you until the time is right. Magical help is not intended to take the place of your own efforts.

Magical letters can be written to any of the Ruling Angels but only on matters He rules, and on His day, you need to invoke or banish.

Do not complicate this system beyond what is given, as the letter is sufficient. Simplicity is the beauty of this art; the Voice of Angels is not a ritual system, just add the knowledge to what you already have.

> 'May the Throne Angel Uri'el grant
> and bless your request'

Path to Uri'el

What you will need:
Oil of frankincense, incense, charcoal, goblet of wine/beer, fruit juice or water, a blue and a green candle, a statue or picture of the angel (optional but very useful).

Preparation:
Don your white robe and tie a deep blue cord around your waist. This will be in respect for the Angel you will be working with. Anoint wrists, temples and throat with oil of frankincense. Light candles. Prepare charcoal and add incense as required. Fill goblet with liquid and raise it in salutation to the angels and place it back on your altar.

Sit comfortably in an upright chair and inhale very slowly and deeply. You are not just inhaling air, but joy, serenity, strength, vitality, courage, and whichever positive quality you want to affirm. Imagine the breath filling not only your lungs, but also the whole body – starting from the feet and culminating at a point between the eyebrows.

As you exhale not only do you expel carbon dioxide from your system, but also mental and emotional impurities such as weakness, discouragement and despair. Feel the intimate connection between the mind and the breath. Feel the flow of energy around your body as you prepare for your ritual working.

Say the temple prayer to the angels:

I call upon thy sacred name

Of the being that has been with me

Since the beginning of beginnings.

As I gaze upwards

May I behold thy beauty and thy splendour unto eternity,

Time without end.

Build your gate with love and care; visualise Angel Hair quartz crystal the colour of citrine pushing up through the earth, towering above your head and disappearing into the heavens. Visualise a brilliant shaft of light pass through it. You stand and marvel at the smoky golden brown strands tipped with red sparks of colour as spirits dance within, then all changes as their brilliant little lives turn an opaque powder blue; other life-forms exist inside. Noticing this sends a sudden shiver through your body.

'Much mystery and magic lay within this cell, Pilgrim.' Luc'ifer says, making a grand sweep through the air with his left hand bringing forth ten crystal walls from the abyss, as they tower above you inner voices ring out: 'All man is Divine' – feel the words within your heart.

All eyes are on you; Mikh'ael, Gabri'el, Sama'el, Rapha'el, Zadki'el, Ana'el and Cassi'el.

'Touch the ninth cell Pilgrim, it is time to call forth the Archangel Uri'el,' orders, Luc'ifer.

It is icy cold beneath your fingers, and you briefly hesitate, but the surface slowly melts for you and Luc'ifer to pass through.

Pause before beginning your invocation. Visualise each word as you utter it. Breathe it into life; endow it with passion and sincerity. Each is a rhythmic element combining to form a powerful symphony, imbue your call with such beauty that the angelic being cannot but help to respond. Not only will you be invoking Uri'el, but going on a journey into the centre of his realm. You will learn how to focus on his energy as you are drawn in. This is your gateway.

'Great Teaching Angel

Defender of the Earth,

Angel of great magic,

Angel of Prayer, Love, Joy and Light

Thou who stands in the presence of God,

Great Throne Angel who art in the Third Heaven,

Protector of Nature Spirits,

Protector against thunder and lightning

Ruler of the Southern River

Receive me into your realm.

Open my heart and my mind

That I may feel you, and know you.

Watcher of the South

I pray thee, show me a sign.'

An unseen hand writes Archangel Uri'el on one of the cell walls.

Uri'el

oo-RE-EL

Commit it to memory. This symbol is charged, look at each mark and take it within.

As you step forward the ice-covered ground crackles beneath your feet. This is Uranus; it has the coldest planetary atmosphere in the Solar System. All around you is a complex layered cloud structure; the lowest clouds are made up of water and the uppermost layer of pure methane, odourless but highly dangerous. The gas wafts upwards creating a fabulous aquamarine colour corona that drifts out to the eleven rings that play host to the acting shepherd moons Cordelia and Ophelia.

The surface of the ground begins to break and through the cracks spring white Bryony plants that tower ten feet into the air, their thick dirty white fleshy tuberous roots split open and ooze out a sickening milky juice; the stench makes you cover your nose and mouth with your hand. Flapping against your face are branching stems that bear glossy green heart-shaped leaves.

Pokeweed plants, fourteen feet high do battle for available space; from their pinkish-red stems sprout emerald green leaves and greenish-white flowers that droop with the weight of clusters of shiny purplish-black berries. A dragonfly enters the scene, and in the space of only minutes you watch an almost transparent body become a metallic green then blue, iridescent red to orange all controlled by the interference of light touching the tiny surfaces of the insects body. Luc'ifer begins to clear a pathway through the Bryony and Pokeweed plants and indicates that you follow him. But curiously, each step you take through the undergrowth stirs the earth bringing up luscious smells of mango and banana. At the edge of the clearing you come to a pool of glistening oil; the surface shimmers with unimaginable colours beyond the spectrum.

Around its edge grow hydrangeas; their mop-head flowers resembling pom-poms; a truly magical plant that suddenly changes shade along with a chameleon that has nestled amongst the petals.

Conjuration

I … (utter your secret name) salute thee and conjure thee,

O beautiful Uranus,

O most beautiful Planet,

By the methane clouds above me,

By the strange gases around me,

O Throne of Auphanim

Who maketh his angels spirits, and

His ministers a flaming fire

By the planet name of Mazlot

By you, O resplendent One, appear!

I conjure thee.

Grace my eyes with your presence

Archangel Uri'el, appear before me!

The scent of jasmine and Musk is all around you. Drink in the aroma Pilgrim, and say:

'Hail Uri'el!

I thank thee for these magical signs.

Around me is heady scent of your presence

I pray that with each intake of breath,

These aromas will serve to intensify my awareness of thee.'

Pause to allow your conscious mind to take in events so far, let it become like a mirror, reflecting, but allowing light through the stillness of powder blue skies above.

A cry suddenly wells up in your throat as you say:

Bless-ed be He,

Bless-ed be the Archangel

Bless-ed be He

Hail Great One! Hail Uri'el!

Thou who now stands before me

Thou whose face is youthful

Upon your proud brow radiates the mark of Uranus ♅

Black is your hair and streaked with grey

Thou who has the sharpest sight in all of Heaven

Powerful is the force of your body clad in robes of deepest blue

Commanding is your right hand that holds a crystal tipped wand

I bow before thee

Thou who sees and knows the vision of the Creator's face

I pray that your eyes look kindly upon me.'

Uri'el smiles down at you, his brown eyes burn bright. The crystal tip of his wand glows, creating a rainbow that spirals in all its splendour up into the atmosphere forming the seal of Uranus; The Grand Seal of the Earth.

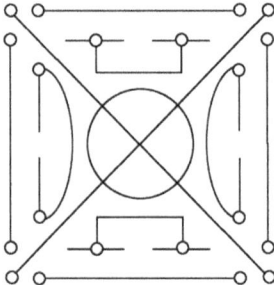

From the heavens the movement of the outer planets begin to harmonise so perfectly together they generate sound waves that spread in great ripples throughout the cosmos. Luc'ifer clasps his hands together in delight; his eyes too are bright and sparkling. There's much magic in the air.

A movement from behind you, followed by a loud high pitched whinny makes you turn around suddenly; standing majestically in front of you is a snowy-white unicorn! He quietly strides closer and bends his head down for you to touch his glistening platinum tipped horn. His eyes tell you much, look deep into his eyes Pilgrim, and see your future. He lowers his head more so that his nose nuzzles in your hand; you feel such warmth and tenderness that evokes a sense of heavenly peace to your heart.

From the clumps of hydrangeas scuttles the chameleon. You stand fascinated by the multi-colour display as its body changes shades and then in a flash the reptile turns into a double-sided tablet.

10	92	3	97	5	96	94	8	99	1
11	19	83	14	86	85	17	88	12	90
80	22	28	74	25	26	77	23	79	71
31	69	33	37	65	66	34	68	62	40
51	42	58	44	46	45	57	53	49	60
50	52	48	54	56	55	47	43	59	41
61	39	63	67	36	35	64	38	32	70
30	72	78	27	75	76	24	73	29	21
81	89	18	84	16	15	87	13	82	20
100	9	93	7	95	6	4	98	2	91

The numbers vibrate and impact upon your senses, feel the numbers within as they hum:

'Inside this square are divine names, Pilgrim, sacred to Uri'el through Uranus – the names of the Intelligence and Spirit, that will one day be revealed.'

Uri'el raises his crystal tipped wand, bestowing a blessing upon you.

Your guardian Luc'ifer takes you by your hand and tells you it is time to leave the angelic realm of Uri'el.

Pilgrim, reflect on what you have uttered, what has been said to you and foremost, what has been revealed. Ask yourself: 'Has this experience changed me?'

Close your eyes and when you open them say these words:

'Eternal are the Archangels and Angels whose celestial realms endureth, forever and ever. I return thanks unto the Great Creator, in Whose Name thou, Uri'el hast come. Depart hence in peace unto thine habitations, and be thou ready to return when so ever I shall have need of thee.'

Utter your secret name to the angels, go through the portal into your world and seal the door behind you.

>'May the Archangel Uri'el guard
>and bless you and keep you safe'

10
Enoch
and the Watchers

Legend

The name Enoch means 'Initiated' and comes from the verb 'hanak' meaning to dedicate, to begin, with one exception (Proverbs 22:6), *'hanak'* and its derivates refer to an action in connection to a building (1 Kings 8:63), wall (Nehemiah 12:27), an altar (Numbers 7:10).

In the Hebrew and Chaldean Lexicon to The Old Testament includes additional meanings: of imprint, pierce into, instruct, make wise. Derivatives are *'hanik'* trained servant (Genesis 14:14) *'hanukka'*, dedication (Psalm 30:title). This noun reappears as the name Hanukkah also known as the Festival of Lights, an eight-day celebration of the re-dedication of the Holy Temple.

Enoch son of Jared appears in Genesis as the seventh of the ten pre-Deluge Patriarchs and is portrayed as the great^{x4} grandson of Adam, through Seth and is described as Methuselah's father, and great-grandfather of Noah (Genesis 5:22-29).

The role of the Patriarchs is chiefly to mark the passage of immense periods of time. Each of the Patriarchs appears to have lived for several centuries, has a son, lives more centuries, and eventually dies. But Enoch is special in this sequence on two counts: his lifespan is exceptionally short compared to his long-lived peers, and Enoch does not die, according to the Bible texts 'he walked with God, he was not, for God took him.' (Genesis 5:22-29).

There are three apocryphal works accredited to Enoch:

1st Book of Enoch, an apocryphal book in the Ethiopic Bible usually dated between the 3rd century and 1st century CE

2nd Book of Enoch an apocryphal book in the Old Slavonic Bible usually dated to the 1st century CE

3rd Book of Enoch, a Kabbalistic Rabbinic text in Rashi (early Hebrew) usually dated to the 5th century CE

These give an account of how Enoch is taken up to Heaven and is chosen as guardian of all the celestial treasures, head of the archangels, and the direct attendant on the Great Creator's throne.

Enoch is taught all the secrets and mysteries and, with the support of the angels, he acts upon all that is uttered by the Great Creator. The prophet was also perceived as a teacher of astronomy, mathematics, and the inventor of writing; all three reflecting the interpretation of his name, further reinforcing the meaning *'initiated'*.

A great deal of esoteric literature as in the 3rd Book of Enoch identifies him as Metatron, the angel that conveys the word of the Great Creator. As a result of this literature and the ancient Kabbalah of Jewish mysticism, Enoch was seen as having been the one who communicated the Great Creator's revelation to Moses, in particular, the one who dictated the Book of Jubilees.

During the time Christianity was separating itself from Judaism, the most popular view of Enoch was that of Targum Yerushalmi (Jerusalem Targum) that regarded him as a pious man who was taken to Heaven and received the title *Safra Rabba (Great scribe)* but then Enoch was abruptly removed from Heaven before he was corrupted.

According to Shlomo Yitzhaki, better known by the acronym Rashi: 'Enoch was a righteous man, but he could easily be persuaded to return to do evil. Therefore, the Holy One, blessed be He, hastened and took him away and caused him to die before his time. For this reason, Scripture changed [the wording] in [the account of] his demise and wrote, 'and he was no longer' in the world to complete his years.'

In one of the mystical writings accredited to Rabbi Ishmael ben Elisha; randomly referred to by a variety of names of *Sefer Hekalot* describes the Rabbi as having visited the 7th Heaven, where he met Enoch, who claimed that earth had, in this time, been corrupted by the demons Shemyaza and Azazel. Hence, Enoch was taken to Heaven to prove that the Great Holy one was not cruel.

Similar traditions are documented in *Wisdom of Sirach* and later versions regarded Enoch as having been a pious ascetic, preached repentance and gathered (despite the small number of people on Earth) a great assembly of disciples, to the extent that he was declared king.

Under Enoch's wise guidance, peace is said to have reigned on Earth, and in front of a vast crowd, Enoch ascends to Heaven on a horse, where he is appointed to rule over the Sons of God.

We now move onto Enoch and the Watchers also known as Grigori. The word 'Grigori' is a transliteration of the Greek word, egregoroi, to mean 'watchers' and is the collective name for a group of angels who lost or fell from grace.

The story of the Nephilim is recorded more fully in the Book of Enoch (part of Ethiopian biblical canon). Enoch, as well as Jubilees, links the origin of the Nephilim with the fallen angels, and in particular with the Watchers (Grigori). Shemyaza, an angel of high rank, is described as leading a rebel sect of angels in a descent to earth to instruct humans in righteousness. The guardianship went on for a number of centuries, but the Watchers changed, and took on the role as teaching man subjects such as; astrology, divination and herb craft, subjects that had been kept secret and considered to be forbidden by the Great Creator.

To make matters worse, the Watchers hungered after the earth women they were supposed to be guiding, and began instructing the women in magic and trickery. The angels consummated their lust, and as a result, the women produced hybrid offspring: the Nephilim; savage giants who pillage the earth and endangered humanity.

Although religious bodies may argue that angels have no gender, and therefore are incapable of procreating, The Watchers story in Enoch is derived from Genesis chapter 6. Verses 1-4 describe the 'Origin of the Nephilim' and mention the 'Sons of God' who beget them:

'When men began to multiply on earth and daughters were born to them, the sons of God saw how beautiful the daughters of man were, and so they took for their wives as many of them as they chose. Then the Lord said: "My spirit shall not remain in man forever, since he is but flesh. His days shall comprise one hundred and twenty years." At that time the Nephilim appeared on earth (as well as later), after the sons of God had intercourse with the daughters of man, who bore them sons. They were the heroes of old, the men of renown.'

Due to this bad angelic behaviour, the Grigori or Watchers were removed from their place of duty and bound 'in the valleys of the Earth' until Judgment Day. Of course the Watchers pleaded with Enoch to speak on their behalf to the Great Creator, but the Holy One's decision could not be swayed.

According to the scriptural texts, the fallen angels who begat the Nephilim were cast into Gehenna a place of torment and suffering where condemned souls exist in total darkness. Jude 1:6:

'And the angels who kept not their first estate, but left their own habitation, he hath reserved in everlasting chains under darkness unto the judgment of the great day.'

But what of the Nephilim? It has been suggested that one of the main reasons for the great deluge, was not to discipline man, but to purify the Earth of these half-breeds created from the union of fallen spirit and flesh. The Book of Jubilees (sometimes called Lesser Genesis) describes the origin of angels and the story of how a group of fallen angels mated with mortal females, giving rise to a race of giants known as the Nephilim. The great flood destroyed their hybrid children, the Nephilim, that were in existence during the time of Noah.

On the other hand, Biblical references to the Nephilim continue after the flood, and can be found in Numbers, Deuteronomy, and Joshua. The antediluvian Nephilim are referred to as

'Anakim' or 'Rephaim'. (As in Num. 13:33, which refers to the sons of Anak as 'Nephilim'.) These references do not necessarily contradict the account of the original Nephilim being completely destroyed in the Deluge. However, Jubilees does state that God granted ten percent of the ethereal spirits of the Nephilim to remain after the flood as demons to attempt to lead the human race astray through idolatry and the occult, until the final Judgement.

The Ethiopian version states that the 'angels' were in fact the disobedient offspring of Seth (Deqiqa Set), and the 'mortal females' were daughters of Cain. This is the view held by most of the earliest critics.

This brings us back to the term 'fallen angel' that is in fact a metaphor for 'casted out' or ostracized.

During the early stellar cults of Mesopotamia there were four 'royal' stars known as the Lords, or the Watchers. Each of these stars 'ruled' over one of the four cardinal points familiar to astrology. This particular system dates from around 3000 BCE.

The star Aldebaran, when it marked the Vernal Equinox, held the position of Watcher of the East.

Regulus, marking the Summer Solstice,
was Watcher of the South.

Antares, marking the Autumn Equinox,
was Watcher of the West.

Fomalhaut, marking the Winter Solstice,
was Watcher of the North.

In the star myths each Watcher was portrayed as a god who guarded the Heavens and the Earth. The over-taking of lunar followed by solar cults replaced the older stellar cults, altered their character as well as the 'status' of the Watchers. Finally the Greeks reduced the Watchers to gods of the four winds.

Early Hebrew mystical sects organized the Watchers, into an Archangel hierarchy known as Rapha'el, Mikh'ael, Gabri'el, and Uri'el. There is reference in the Old Testament (Dani'el 4: 13 17) made to the Irin, or Watchers, that seem to be an order of angels.

The most common associations found in various texts on medieval magic regard the Watchers as an evil class of fallen angels known as the 'principalities of the air'. St. Paul, in the New Testament, calls the Fallen Angels 'principalities': 'for we are not contending against flesh and blood, but against the principalities, against the powers...against the spiritual hosts of wickedness in High Places'. It was also St. Paul who called Satan 'The prince of power of the air', and thus made the connection of Satan (himself connected to 'a star', Isaiah 14: 12-14) and etheric beings, for they were later known as demons and as principalities of the Air.

In the Wiccan system, the Watchers, or 'Lords of the Watchtowers' are beings that guard the four portals linking worlds together. These Watchers are looked upon as a spiritual race, a set of deities, and spirits of the four elements associated with the four quarters; east, south, west and north; together with the four elements, air, fire, water and earth. They are also linked to each solstice and equinox as well as a particular star or planet.

Charles Leland - Folklorist and Author, whose 19th Century field studies in Italy, exposed the existence of a surviving Witch Cult from ancient times.

In his book *Aradia*, or the *Gospel for Witches* published, 1899, in 'The Children of Diana', Charles tells an intriguing story about how fairies were born and states that Diana created 'the great spirits of the stars'. Another fable is titled 'How Diana made the Stars and the Rain' where Diana went 'to the mothers and fathers of the Beginning; the spirits who were before the first spirit'. According to some Italian witches this reference alleges that the Watchers (Grigori) were from this ancient race.

It is the practise of Wiccans to call down the Watchers at the quarterly 'Watchtowers' to guard and witness the rites performed before them, beginning in the east; the practitioner traces an invoking Earth Pentagram while uttering:

'Ye Lords of the Watchtowers of the East, ye Lords of Air; I do summon, stir and call you up, to witness these rites and to guard our Circle.'

During initiation into Wicca each new initiate is introduced to the Watchers in the four quarters.

'Take heed, O Lords of the Watchtowers of the East, (name), properly prepared, will be made a Priestess and a Witch.'

Many Gardnerian and later Alexandrian covens used the archangel's names, and as the Neo-Pagan movement developed, foundation beginnings tended to grow away from Biblical sources. Many covens had no set names for the so-called Mighty Ones of the Four Directions, or Lords of the Watchtowers, the Old Ones and Dread Lords of the Outer Spaces. But whatever name is used, the Watchers are important to the Witchcraft and Wiccan traditions as they are not only the guardians of the portal to other realms, but also protectors of the magic circle, and witnesses to rites. In Ancient times a 'Tower' was a military fighting unit, and a 'Watchtower' was a defending home unit, similar to a National Guard. So, each of the ruling Watchers oversees a Watchtower, which is now a portal marking one of the four quarters of the ritual circle.

'Hence the perfection of the universe requires that there should be intellectual creatures. Now to understand cannot be the action of a body, nor of any corporeal power.... Hence the perfection of the universe requires the existence of an incorporeal creature.'
Summa Theologiae 1a, 50, 1

Path to Enoch

What you will need:
Oil of frankincense, incense, charcoal, goblet of wine/beer, fruit juice or water, two white candles, a picture of the firmament of heaven.

Preparation:
Don your white robe and tie a white cord around your waist. This will be in respect for the energies you will be working with. Anoint wrists, temples and throat with oil of frankincense. Light two white candles. Prepare charcoal and add incense as required. Fill goblet with liquid and raise it in salutation to the angels and place it back on your altar.

Sit comfortably in an upright chair and inhale very slowly and deeply. You are not just inhaling air, but joy, serenity, strength, vitality, courage, and whichever positive quality you want to affirm. Imagine the breath filling not only your lungs, but also the whole body – starting from the feet and culminating at a point between the eyebrows.

As you exhale not only do you expel carbon dioxide from your system, but also mental and emotional impurities such as weakness, discouragement and despair. Feel the intimate connection between the mind and the breath. Feel the flow of energy around your body as you prepare for your ritual working.

Say the temple prayer to the angels:

I call upon thy sacred names

Of the beings that have been with me

Since the beginning of beginnings.

As I gaze upwards

May I behold thy beauty and thy splendour unto eternity,

Time without end.

Build your gate with love and care; visualise Angel Hair quartz crystal the colour of citrine pushing up through the earth, towering above your head and disappearing into the heavens. Visualise a brilliant shaft of light pass through it. Marvel at the smoky golden brown strands tipped with red sparks of colour as spirits dance within. Feel the cool of moonbeams as you pass through the gleaming portal. You are unnerved as again you stand on a ten-edged crystal platform knowing full well that the yawning abyss is far below. The ten crystal cell walls materialize before you, each with the ghost image of an angel. Haunting voices call, but who are they calling? The sounds disappear into the depths of a dank mist that rises in great swirls around you. You hear a low whisper:

'I have a tale to tell you Pilgrim… I have a tale to tell. Follow the pathway yonder.'

Beneath your feet are worn and weathered cobbles. You feel the cold harsh breath of winter on your face. Briefly the mist clears revealing a tall gaunt figure wearing a black-feathered cape. Fear grips you as the silent shape pauses, turns around, and fixes you with his bluish- pink eyes!

Your legs tremble making it difficult for you to stand – briefly you recover, giving you enough time to take refuge in a doorway. Above your head is a sign that reads: I bid thee welcome.

What strange mystery have you happened upon? Who can say what phantasms fill the brains of man? A voice says: 'Enter in, I bid thee welcome.'

All is dark inside the chamber. You strain your eyes trying to make out the objects in this room. Books line the high walls, many books and many titles, all holding a mystery within their covers.

You reach out your hand and select a book; the title is concealed beneath decades of dust. Open the tome of mystery Pilgrim and read the words of wisdom:

'In the days that are forgotten,

In the unremembered ages,

Lived a man whose mind was opened,

He alone could talk to angels.'

Raise your eyes and say:

'O that I could speak to this one.'

A strange mist envelops your being blotting out all around you. Through the vapour you detect a doorway. What trick is this? A tendril-like mist coils about you, waving like a beckoning hand. A rush of wings and a cry of voices disturb the air shaking the ground beneath your feet.

'Who art thou who cries around me?'

They eerily reply:

'We are the spirits now departed, souls of those who were once with you. Go in search of Prophet Enoch! Ask the questions, find the answers. He alone can talk to angels, may your wishes serve to guide you.'

Walk through the doorway Pilgrim, follow fast those heavy footprints along a pathway so well trodden. May your life be changed forever!

This is no ordinary path. A feeling of weakness and a loss of balance makes you reach out to grab for something to hold on to, but you are in a void. Suddenly, a sensation of weightlessness overcomes you sending you catapulting, free-falling backwards through space and time. Fabulous colours beyond the spectrum speed past you, arcs of light dazzle you, crystalline sounds so pure implode to your core, invigorating your senses. You have arrived Pilgrim, back to the Age of Watchers.

There, you find him in a temple. Enoch stands gazing upwards, bathed in a golden light so splendid; he is glorious. From his proud head to his shoulders fall grey-white silken tresses. He is clothed in the richest of garments, silks, ermine, and the finest of wools.

You approach him in reverence, and say:

'I pray thee Enoch,

Tell me a story, of the legend and traditions,

After the creation of the heavens.'

The old man turns to you, sadness and sorrow in his grey eyes. A heavy cloud overhangs the atmosphere casting dark shadows on the ground around you. Enoch raises his hands up and speaks:

'I shall answer, I shall tell you.

I am he whose eyes were opened

To see Holy visions in the heavens.

All of this the Angels showed me.

Of the turmoil on Mount Hermon,

And destruction of old Ardis.

And the thunder and the lightning.

'Then the Angels spake more clearly:

''It is not for you, these words of warning,

But a distant generation!'

Enoch gazed upward, speaking:

'The Holy Great One left his high place.

I walked with Him upon this earth-plane.

He warned me of the times of trouble.'

'Listen carefully, wisest Enoch,

I bequeath to all those chosen,

Joy and insight, and life triumphant

Thus my wrath shall not attain them

And my vengeance shall not reach them?

'But for those, for those transgressors,

I heap a curse!

They shall be a tribe accurs-ed!

Fall and fade and die and wither!

Numbered are their lives on this plane.'

'But what of me O Holy Great One?'

Darkness is replaced by a burst of light that shines forth upon Enoch; just being with him fills you with overwhelming emotion. Within this golden light is a sound. A voice:

'Wise and humble art thou Enoch,

Thou wilt be spared amongst the many.

Fear not Enoch! For thou art Bless-ed.'

Pause to allow your conscious mind to take in events so far, let it become like a river flowing always towards enlightenment. Take a deep breath and say:

Tell me more, I pray thee, tell me.'

From the lips of prophet Enoch, legend-teller, story-maker:

'From the rising of Mount Hermon,

Who many call it 'Mount of Curses,

From the great skies to the heavens,

From the wilderness and marsh-lands,

Where the vulture god, Ver-eth-ragna

Feeds among the dead and dyeing.'

He gives you a look so sad and dismal, the golden glow around him is wiped away and replaced by storm clouds sailing onward, spreading over all the sky. A distant rumbling of thunder then lightning quivers, followed by a silent darkness. Enoch speaks:

'This is what the Angels showed me,

This is what the bird-ones told me.

Great Mount Hermon *will* be shaken,

And the high hills will be laid low,

They will melt like wax in fire

And the earth will shake and tremble.

All you see will be destroy-ed,

Then there'll be a final judgment,

Upon the righteous and the wicked.'

A chilled wind flurries around you making you shiver. The prophet continues:

'From the mists of great Mount Hermon,

Came a race of massive beings,

They were giants among the earth-man,

Shining, hawk-like were their features,

Blue-Pinkish eyes and snow-white tresses,

All were dressed in vulture feathers,

Capes so long, sweeping swishing.

'We all knew them as the Watchers.

All man were fearful of the Watchers,

And the lineage of the Watchers,

Then the Watchers spoke together

In a tongue that was so foreign:

'See the daughters of the earth-man,
See the beauty of these women,
Let's choose us wives among these maidens,
They are fair,
They'll bear our children!
May our hearts and bodies join together.'

Enoch weeps, from his eyes tears are flowing like the melting snows of Mount Hermon. His body shakes and trembles as he sobs out the words:

'I beheld these fearsome marches
Of these unknown awesome creatures.
Lord Shemyaza was their leader.
Cried Shemyaza in a voice of thunder,
In a tone of loud derision,
Scolded thus his wayward brothers:

'You'll bring the wrath of gods upon us!
Let us hasten back to Hermon'

Like the vultures on the crag-tops, laughing at his condemnation, laughed and shouted all together:

'Hasten back? O Shemyaza!
We'll hasten back to find these women!
Hush Shemyaza! Your words we hear not!
Do not think that we believe them!'

The brothers muttered all together:

'Take no notice of our leader,

He is jealous of our power

Let us sign a pact together,

Let us all mate with these fair maidens!'

Enoch indicates that you walk with him, and together you go further back through time. He continues his tale with a steady voice:

'And all bound one to another,

Swore with curses to each other,

Disregarding wise Shemyaza.

'Then, they all massed together,

And they numbered twice one hundred,

Down they swarmed upon old Ardis,

Swarming in great hordes from Hermon,

Led by leaders named as follows:

Rami-el, Kokabi-el, and Ura-kiba

Dani-el, Ezeqi-el, and Arm-ar-os,

Baraqi-el, Ana-el, and Samsi-el,

Sata-el, Turi-el, and Ara-zi-el.

Azaz-el, Yomi-el, and Tam-i-el

Zaqi-el was the last to join them.

Known as Angels by the earth-man.'

You both descend down a narrow path that overlooks a beautiful valley. A rock over hang provides a suitable resting place for the ancient man, and together you sit. Enoch heaves a heavy sigh and continues:

'Thus the earth-man sang together

In one voice for all to listen:

Let us welcome these tall strangers,

Hail them as our friends and brothers,

Show them our right hand of friendship.'

Said this to me, wise old Enoch:

'I beheld too in a vision

All the secrets of the future,

Of the distant days that shall be.'

Enoch pauses, closing his eyes. The fatigue of ages is imprinted on his brow. He speaks in a low voice:

'So the Watchers taught them mystery.

Revealed the secrets known in Heaven.

Azaz-el taught the men forge-working,

Swords and daggers, shields and breast-plates.

Showed them how to make fine jewel'ry,

Ornaments for hair and body.

Thus the women put on make-up,

Painted colour on their faces,

Adorned their hair with many gemstones.

Ura-kiba taught earth-men magick,

How to use the herbs and tree roots,

Chant the songs to cure all illness.

Wandered eastward, wandered westward,

Teaching men the art of herb-lore,

And the antidotes for poisons,

And the curing of diseases.

Thus was first made known to mortals

All the sacred art of healing,

And the mystery of the Watchers.

Even to the dullest of us, the spirit world always seems closer under a night sky; our perception of things becomes more sensitive to previous unfelt sensations, even hard shapes take on ghostly outlines.

The night sky is now purple-indigo, a mystic colour that suits our pathworking well. The stars are increasing in number forming a marvellous dome above your head. The moon too has strengthened his contribution to light up the spectral scene around you. Enoch smiles, and with renewed energy, he continues:

'Baraqi-el, Tami-el knew the night-sky,

Of the orbs that shine in heaven,

They did teach the earth-folk star-lore.

Of the moon-lore Azaz-el taught them

Learnt the phases of this planet.

The world was changing fast around them,

Gone respect and preservation,

Hailing disrespect and fornication.

'Next the Watchers sought the maidens,

Saw them dance and craved their bodies.

Made the women wanton creatures,
Sought them out for carnal pleasure.
Seeded them and planted monsters!
How they suffered in childbearing,
Birthing babes who split their bellies,
Still they lusted for their loving,
Turning from the love of earth-men.

Earth-men toiled and laboured for them,
Day and night they slaved and suffered,
But the Watchers were too greedy,
Thus they shouted, screamed at earth-man:
'Not enough! We need more feeding!
Gather up the wheat and barley,
Pick the ripe fruits from the orchards,
Catch the fish from all the rivers,
Slaughter all the sheep and cattle!'

'But my lords, we are near starving!'

'Hush your mouths, worthless earth-men,
We care not about your bellies!
Just leave the foods outside our dwelling,
Be gone now for we seek our pleasure!'

The food then gone, their bellies empty,
Watchers ate the flesh of humans.

Sinning now against all nature,

Turning then on one another.

A creeping blackness covers the sky sending the stars into the darkness of the unknown. You shiver and take comfort knowing Enoch is beside you. He is now struggling to continue as visions of the past come back to haunt him. He looks straight into your eyes and says:

'Man cried out to all the old ones,

Their voices reached the Gate of Heaven,

'Help us please we beg you, help us!

Look upon us, and our women,

See how they all quickly perish

They give birth to monstrous beings

Who then devour our very bodies!'

'The Gods looked down upon this rabble,

Heard the cries of earth-men clearly.

The Great Holy One's voice boomed loudly:

'I will send My finest Angels!

To rid the Watchers from your earth-plane.

'Azaz-el revealed the secrets!

Secrets that belong in Heaven!

'Ura-kiba taught earth-men magick,

Shemyaza! Hear me clearly

I will banish you forever!

You will wander on the earth-plane,
No soul-mate will keep you company!'

Enoch looked serious, and pointed skyward saying:
'There was a splitting in the heavens,
Thunder, lightning and fiery flashes,
Rolling black clouds heaving sideways,
Hailstones pounded on the Watchers,
Fire singed and burnt their cloaks of feathers,
Turned their fair and snowy skin black.

'How they screamed and screamed for mercy,
Massive giant forms swaying madly,
Many ran into the waters,
Others made into the forest.

'Earth-men hid within the caverns.
Whilst the old earth shook around them,
'What have we done?' they cried together.
Then the Great voice boomed above them:
'I have done what you have asked me.'

Silence reigned on earth's old kingdom, then a parting of the heavens revealed a vision O so splendid; shafts of golden light fell downwards like a marvellous but swift sunset. You glimpse a dazzling angel as it hovers above; his quivering halo is coloured in every hue from gold to red. The light suffuses with so many tints that overwhelm you into ecstatic absorption.

Trumpets sound, voices ring out heralding the four archangels: Raph-a-el floats earthwards, followed closely by Mikha'el, Gabri'el now settles softly, then finally Uri'el, the tallest of them.

When they see the mass of bloodshed, and the wickedness of Watchers, and the evilness of these giants, thus they say to one another:

'Let us shout this crime forever!

Hear earth's cry of devastation

Right up to the Gates of Heaven.'

Rapha'el of air, steps forward youthful, spring-like, healer doctor:

'I, Archangel of joy and laughter,

I shall guard the Eastern Portal

Placed in Hod, glory and splendour'

Mikha'el of fire salutes:

'I stand for justice, strength and safety,

I shall guard the Southern Portal,

I am young, with fiery temper

Placed in Tiphareth, harmony and beauty.'

Gabri'el of water drifts forward, man of middle age, and wisdom:

'I stand for mercy, peace and rebirth,

I shall guard the Western Portal,

Placed in Yesod, Thy Foundation.'

Uri'el of earth comes forward, an elderly man with crystal vision!

'I, the Angel of lightning, storms and thunder,

Shall guard the Northern Portal,
I hold the rainbow, font of knowledge,
Placed in Mal-kuth, Thy Kingdom.'

Thus their voices rang together till the earth-plane shook and rumbled. Chanted singly and in chorale, mystic were the songs they chanted:
'We will always stay on earth's plane
Protectors of the temple quarters.'

Thus a temple built around them,
Thus assembled these four angels.'

'Then what happened I beseech thee?'

Enoch answered, hands uplifted:
'I stood within this temple centre,
Rapha'el thus stood before me,
Gabri'el then stood behind me,
Mikha'el to *the* right of me,
And Uri'el to *the* left of me.

A white light then shone all around me,
Mikha'el placed a dagger on me
Touched my forehead lightly saying
Aah-taah - Thou Art, Enoch!'

'On my heart the dagger rested

Light now penetrated from it

Mal-kuth – Thou art The Kingdom, Enoch!'

Touching lightly my right shoulder:
've-Geburah, and the Power, Enoch!'

Touching lightly my left shoulder:
've-Gedulah, and the Glory, Enoch!'

'Then I clasped my hands together

Light cascaded all around me.'

As you listen to wise Enoch, a great light forms around you, the Great One of Heaven stands before you and raises His hands in benediction. He speaks the words of El-Shaddai issuing vowel sounds in a strange tongue, that continue on forever.

Your head now fills with soul sounds opening all your centres; from the crown to your bare feet. Like a tree of life now growing, each part of your body lights up just resembling the No-thing the Great Creator hailed from. You see a tree formation and the many orbs of colour, each one spinning out of chaos to an order of a kingdom. You can hear voices calling, but they are not speaking directly to you, just making harmonious sounds. All around the sounds vibrate.

Thus you utter up the answers to the many hidden questions. Your heart is bursting with emotion as you speak to the Great One:

'All my heart is carried to you,

All my devotion goes on to you.

I am one, I am with you.'

From your eyes the tears are falling, and He hears the echo of your crying, crying to him from afar off. Held by unseen hands you begin sinking downward through the vacant spaces, downward through the clouds of vapours till you rest on the hearthstone of His temple where you hear a single clear voice saying:

'See yourself not as a stranger,

Not even as a separate being,

But part of my creation.

Although you are a child of this earth,

Your race is from the starry heavens,

Use your body wisely Pilgrim,

Tune yourself to all around you,

You are the Tree of Life Mandala.

Within you now are all the symbols,

Call each one in turn to answer,

Speak in the holy tongue I taught you.'

Take deep breaths and chant, chant through the night till dawning. You are now at one with El-Shaddai, recognised the angels' faces, each one coming from a quarter, say:

'I will learn your names and all your secrets,

I will learn to send you each a message

I will send it singing like a herald,

And, as a bearer of this message,

I *will* speak directly to El-Shaddai.'

In the presence of old Enoch you don the holy golden mitre. Take from an angel the lamen of finest silk and deepest purple. Take the ring of ruby star-fire, don the breastplate of great power, take the golden wand of magic, receive the blessing from the mighty, leave behind your old persona, and emerge as the Pilgrim resplendent and say:

'I clasp my hands together,

I touch my breast, I feel the power,

Thus my blinded eyes are open,

Seeing heaven's holy visions,

Forever, unto the ages.

LE-OLAHM,

AMEN.'

You take in the scene around you, the remnants of the light left behind by the visitation of the Great Creator, and you listen to the ever-weakening echo of your voice as it is absorbed back into the atmosphere around you.

You think of the angels, those ancient beings who both hated and revered their creator, the marvellous changes of light that seeped into your very soul; take all this into your heart. All now dissolves around you, and by your side is Luc'ifer whose smile says it all. Red sparks of light flicker in his amber eyes reminiscent of the spirits that danced within the citrine quartz of the angelic walls.

Stand silently, and think about what you have uttered, what has been said to you and foremost, what has been revealed throughout all your pathworkings. An inner voice asks you Pilgrim: Has this experience changed you? Close your eyes and when you open them say these words:

'Eternal are the Archangels and Angels whose celestial realms endureth, forever and ever. I return thanks unto the Great Creator, in Whose Name thou, Enoch hast come. Depart hence in peace unto thine habitations, and be thou ready to return when so ever I shall have need of thee.'

Utter your secret name to the angels, go through the portal into your world and seal the door behind you.

---o---o---o---o---

Alphabets to use

Theban

The origins of the Theban alphabet are unknown. It was first published by Johannes Trithemius' Polygraphia in 1518, in which it was attributed to 'Honorius of Thebes'. This alphabet bears little resemblance to other alphabets and has not been found in any earlier works prior to Johannes Trithemius.

The Theban alphabet is used by witches to write spells, inscriptions and other texts. It serves to disguise the meaning of a text and to give it a mystical quality and hide magical writings such as the contents of the Book of Shadows from prying eyes.

There is a one-to-one correspondence between letters of the Theban and Latin alphabets with the exception of the letters j, u and w. These letters are represented by the letters for i, v and vv. This system only exists in a single case. The direction of writing is left to right in horizontal lines.

Passing the River or Passage du Fleuve

The origin of Passing the River is derived from the Hebrew alphabet and was created by Heinrich Cornelius Agrippa during the 16th Century. The direction of writing is left to right in horizontal lines.

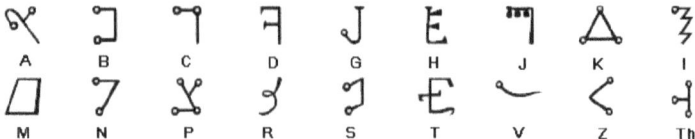

Celestial

The Celestial alphabet, which is also known as the Angelic alphabet, is derived from the Hebrew and Greek alphabets and was created by Heinrich Cornelius Agrippa during the 16th Century and used for communication with angels. Direction of writing: left to right in horizontal lines.

It is not case specific. Capital and lower-case give the same character, except for the S and T keys. Capital 'S' gives Shin, lower-case gives Samech; capital 'T' gives Theth, and lower-case gives Tau

Angel Chart

Planet	Angel	Heaven	Day	Candle	Colour of Cords	Aroma	Metals	Stone
Venus ♀	Lucifer	Sixth	Fri	Red & Black	Gold & Black	Heliotrope, vanilla, amber, myrrh	Aurichalcum	sardius, topaz, carbuncle, adventurine, sapphire, crystal quartz, ligure, white agate & amethyst
Sun ☉	Mikh'ael	Fourth	Sun	Orange	Red	Cinnamon, myrrh, amber	Gold	Diamond
Moon ☾	Gabri'el	First	Mon	White	Silver & Light Blue	Camphor, Jasmine, Frankincense White-Sandalwood	Silver	Pearls Moonstone Mother of Pearl, white agate,
Mars ♂	Sama'el	Fifth	Tue	Red	Orange & Red	Patchouli, Carnation, Sulphur Cardamom, Catmint	Bronze	Ruby Red carbuncle
Mercury ☿	Rapha'el	Third	Wed	Yellow	Yellow & Light Blue	White Sandalwood, Narcissus, Verbena, Chamomile Cinnamon	Quick Silver	Yellow Citrine

Jupiter ♃	Zadki'el	Sixth	Thursday	Purple	Purple	nutmeg, cinnamon, cloves, lilac	Brass & Tin	Amethyst
Venus ♀	Ana'el	Second	Friday	Green	Emerald Green	Roses, Saffron, Verbena, Sandalwood, Myrtle	Copper	Turquoise Emerald
Saturn ♄	Cassi'el	Seventh	Saturday	Black	Black	Mimosa, Myrrh, Patchouli	Platignum & a Mixture of Alloys, lead	Jet
Uranus ♅	Uri'el		Saturday	Blue & Green	Dark Blue	Jasmine, Musk	Platignum & a Mixture of Alloys, lead	Amber

Chart of Angel Hours

1st and 8th hours of the day. 3rd and 10th hours of the night.

00.00 - 01.00 hours		Zadki'el
01.00 - 02.00 hours		Ana'el
02.00 - 03.00 hours		Uri'el
03.00 - 04.00 hours		Cassi'el
04.00 - 05.00 hours		Mikh'ael
05.00 - 06.00 hours		Gabri'el
06.00 - 07.00 hours		Sama'el
07.00 - 08.00 hours		Rapha'el
08.00 - 09.00 hours		Zadki'el
09.00 - 10.00 hours		Ana'el
10.00 - 11.00 hours		Uri'el
11.00 - 12.00 hours		Cassi'el
12.00 - 13.00 hours		Mikh'ael
13.00 - 14.00 hours		Gabri'el
14.00 - 15.00 hours		Sama'el
15.00 - 16.00 hours		Rapha'el
16.00 - 17.00 hours		Zadki'el
17.00 - 18.00 hours		Ana'el
18.00 - 19.00 hours		Uri'el
19.00 - 20.00 hours		Cassi'el
20.00 - 21.00 hours		Mikh'ael
21.00 - 22.00 hours		Gabri'el

22.00 - 23.00 hours   Sama'el
23.00 - 24.00 hours   Rapha'el

Note: According to Peter de Abano, "…. that the first hour of the day, of every Country, and in every season whatsoever, is to be assigned to the Sun-rising, when he first appeareth arising in the horizon: and the first hour of the night is to be the thirteenth hour, from the first hour of the day …." According to occult law a day starts at daybreak, not at midnight

Notes on
The Seal of Truth

SIGILLVM DEI ÆMÆTH: EMETH אמת

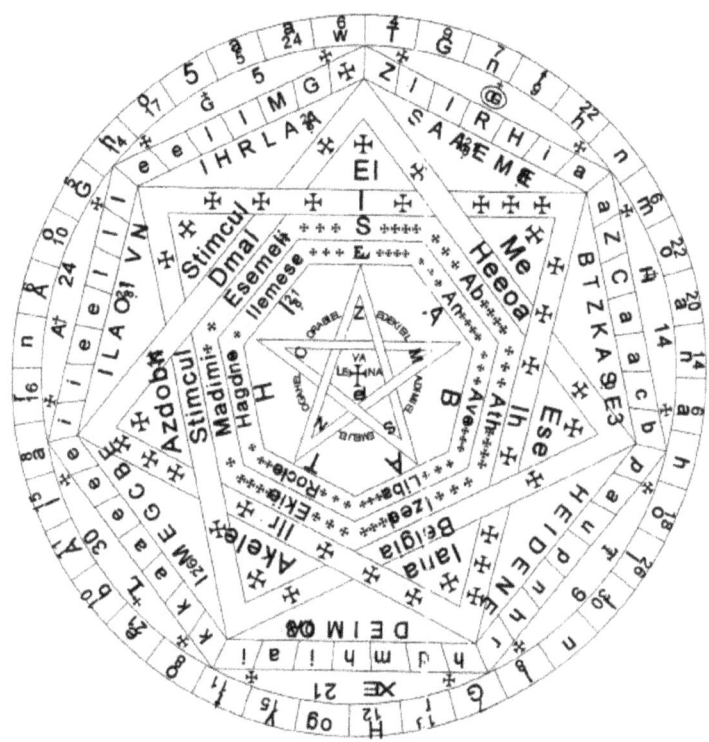

'Thy Character must haue the names of the five Angells (written in the middst of Sigillum AEmath) graven upon the other side in a Circle. In the middst wherof must the stone be (which was allso browght) Wherein, Thow shalt at all tymes Beholde, (privately to thy self) the State of Gods people, throwgh the whole earth. I came across the seal' *De HEPTARCHIA MYSTICA, Doctor Johannes Dee*

Sigillum dei Aemeth: 'Ameth' is Hebrew for 'truth'; hence the Seal of Truth. The actual sigil predates Dr Johannes Dee, having first appeared in a 13th century Grimoire that was later expanded upon by Athanasius Kircher a 17th century German Jesuit scholar.

In 1582, according to Johannes Dee, through his medium Edward Kelley, Dee received the description of the seal. However Johannes Dee's academic interest in the sigil became secondary in favour of more magical pursuits for which he is best known for in relation to his Enochian workings.

During his scrying lessons with Edward Kelly, Dee was instructed by angels to re-create the 'Seal of Truth'. This was in the form of wax disks that were put under each leg of the Holy Table and beneath Kelly's scrying stone. Dee believed that the sigil would protect the magical workings from all outside influences.

Colin Campbell states in *Magic Seal of Dr John Dee*: 'It was this study by that led to my recognition of the Sigillum Dei (of Dee and Kelley) as a cogent magical system in its own right by virtue of the distinct hierarchical cosmology defined in its successive tiers. Yes, it fits into the greater scheme of the Enochian temple with which it was so intimately connected, but it was also valid outside of that context as a planetary system in its own right.'

The British Museum, London possesses numerous items owned by Dee such as; the large richly decorated wax 'Seal of Truth' used to hold the 'shew-stone', the crystal scrying ball; the four small wax seals used to support the legs of the scrying table; the Speculum or mirror an obsidian Aztec magical object in the shape of a hand-mirror, brought to Europe in the late 1520s, that was once owned by Horace Walpole; a gold talisman engraved with an image of one of Kelly's visions; a 2½" diameter crystal ball.

Bibliography

Achtemeier Paul *Harper's Bible Dictionary*, Harper & Row, San Francisco, 1985

Ashley, Leonard. *The Complete Book of Devils and Demons* Skyhorse Publishing, United States, 2011

Author unknown *The Secret Grimoire of Turiel* Translated from the Latin version of 1518

Bamberger, Bernard Jacob, Fallen Angels: Soldiers of Satan's Realm, 2006

Belderis Ina Sunrise magazine, October/November 1996. Theosophical University Press.)

Boyce, J.M. *The Smithsonian Book of Mars*. Old Saybrook, CT: Konecky & Konecky. (2008).

Bunson, Matthew, *Angels A to Z : A Who's Who of the Heavenly Host*. Three Rivers Press. (1996).

Burton Russell Jeffrey *The Early Christian Tradition*, , Cornell University Press, Ithaca, 1991

Carr, Michael H. (2006). *The Surface of Mars*. New York: Cambridge University Press.

Collins Andrew *From Ashes of Angels*

Cambell Colin *The Magic Seal of Dr John Dee, The Sigillum Dei Aemeth* The Teitan Press, York Beach, ME, U.S.A., 2009

Davidson Gustav *A Dictionary of Angels, Including the Fallen Angels.*, The Free Press, New York, 1967

Davies Owen *Grimoires: A History of Magic Books*. Oxford University Press USA 2009

Fox Matthew and Sheldrake Rupert *The Physics of Angels* Harper San Francisco 1996

Ginzberg Louis in *Legend of the Jews* The Johns Hopkins University Press, 1998

Ginzberg Louis *The Ascension of Moses* (Chapter IV - Aggadah - The Legend of The Jews

Glazier, Michael and Hellwig, Monika K.*The Modern Catholic Encyclopedia* Liturgical Press, 2004.

Kitto John *A Cyclopedia of Biblical Literature*, ed., 3rd ed., J. B. Lippincott and Co, Philadelphia, 1866

Leitch Aaron *Secrets of the Magickal Grimoires* Llewellyn Publications, United States, 2005.

Leitch Aaron *The Angelical Language, Volume I: The Complete History and Mythos of the Tongue of Angels:* Llewellyn Worldwide Ltd, 2010

Moore, Patrick *The Data Book of Astronomy*. New York: CRC Press. p. 483. (2000).

New Oxford Annotated Bible (New Revised Standard Version)

Penniuck Nigel *Magical Alphabets* Samuel Weiser, York Beach, Me.: Weiser Books, 1992

Plant David, *Kepler & the Music of the Spheres*

Pope Hugh T, Transcribed by Sean Hyland. *The Catholic Encyclopedia*, Volume VI. Published 1909. New York:

Rhodes Ron, *Angels Among Us*, Harvest House Publishers, 1994

S. L. MacGregor Mathers, A. Crowley, *The Goetia: The Lesser Key of Solomon the King* Samuel Weiser Inc., New York 1904

S. L. MacGregor Mathers, *The Key of Solomon the King* Samuel Weiser Inc., New York 1997

Schwartz, Howard, *Lilith's Cave: Jewish tales of the Supernatural*, San Francisco: Harper & Row, 1988.

Woollet Benjamin *The Queen's Conjuror* Harper Collins, London 2001

Wilson Colin *The Occult*: A History. Random House, 1971

Index

Abraham, 43, 65, 80, 99, 116
Absolute Realm, 37, 38
Abyss, 34, 35, 50, 69, 86, 105, 121, 140, 158, 177
Adonai, 52
Aggadah, 80, 223
Agi'el, 163, 164
Akkadian, 10
Aldebaran, 190
Aleph-Mem-Tav, 60, 76, 112
Alexander the Great, 64
Alexandrian, 192
Almadel of Solomon, 6
Aloes, 56
Amalthea, 122
Amesha Spenta, 11
Amethysts, 125
Ana'el, 15, 81, 133, 134, 135, 136, 137, 139, 140, 141, 142, 143, 144, 146, 147, 149, 150, 166, 177, 216, 217
Anakim, 189
Angel Chart, 22
Angel of annunciation, 64
Angel of Creation, 81
Angel of Revelation, 63
Angel of Sanctification, 169
Angel of the Annunciation, 65
Angelos, 12
Angels, 5
Anoint, 33, 49, 68, 85, 104, 120, 157, 176, 193

Antares, 190
Anthroposophists, 81
Antiochus Epiphanes, 64
Apocryphon, 81
Aquarius, 155, 174
Aqui'el, 55
Araboth, 159
Aralim, 159
Archangel, 13, 27, 32, 33, 35, 36, 40, 41, 43, 46, 47, 48, 49, 51, 54, 55, 56, 58, 59, 63, 65, 66, 67, 69, 70, 72, 74, 75, 76, 77, 78, 79, 83, 84, 86, 87, 88, 90, 91, 92, 96, 97, 102, 103, 105, 106, 108, 109, 111, 112, 114, 115, 118, 119, 122, 123, 124, 125, 126, 127, 128, 129, 131, 133, 135, 137, 140, 141, 143, 144, 146, 147, 149, 150, 151, 153, 155, 156, 158, 159, 161, 162, 163, 164, 165, 169, 171, 173, 174, 175, 177, 178, 180, 183, 190, 206
Archangel of revelation, 65
Archangel of the Holy Sefirot, 63
Archangel of the Moon, 65
Ardis, 196
Aries, 83
Arm-ar-os, 200
Ashmodai, 73
Azazel, 187
Azazye'el, 98
Babylon, 27, 28, 63, 134

Baraqi-el, 200
Bartzabel, 91
Basalt magma, 86
Beech, 160
Bees, 60, 147
Belial, 44
Belladonna, 163
Beryl, 29
Bethor, 126
Bigotry, 46
Black ink, 103
Black Stone of the Kaba, 65
Blue ink, 32, 67, 118, 137
Book of Enoch, 44, 186
Book of Soyga, 13
Book of the Watchers, 171
Botticelli, 100
Brahman, 11
Breaking of Negative Spells, 82
Briah, 81
British Isles, 45
British Museum, 220
Brussels, 45
Bryony, 179
Butterflies, 52
Caduceus, 98, 109, 110, 112
Cairo, 81
Campbell, Colin, 220
Cancer, 66
Candles, 12, 14, 15, 33, 49, 68, 85, 104, 120, 157, 176
Capricorn, 155

Carbon Dioxide, 33, 36, 49, 68, 85, 104, 120, 139, 157, 176, 193
Carnation, 126
Carrier of Light, 27
Cassi'el, 15, 151, 152, 153, 154, 155, 156, 157, 158, 159, 160, 161, 162, 163, 164, 165, 167, 168, 177, 216, 217
Cedar, 126
Celestial, 214
Celestial army, 43
Celestial Script, 174
Chaldean Lexicon, 185
Charcoal, 33, 49, 68, 85, 104, 120, 157, 176
Cherubim, 63, 106, 115
Chief Ambassador to Humanity, 63
Chief of evil spirits, 79
Christians, 11, 28, 64, 99
Circle, 7, 15, 38, 45, 76, 122
Cleansing, 22
Cordelia, 179
Council of Rome, 170
Courage, 33, 45, 49, 56, 68, 75, 82, 83, 85, 92, 104, 111, 120, 127, 157, 163, 176
Covens, 192
Crocodile, 164
Cyprus, 160
Daddy-long legs spiders, 52
Dani'el, 64
Daughters of the Daughters, 20, 149
de Abano, Peter, 218

de Gilvry, Emile Grillot, 152
De Originibus, 13
Dead Sea Scrolls, 43
Dee, Johannes, 12, 13, 172, 220
Deluge, 185, 189
Devas, 11
Devil, 13, 27
Diamond, 29, 35
Diana, 191
Diary, 25
Divine, 5, 6, 13, 36, 38, 40, 46, 50, 52, 57, 58, 60, 75, 86, 92, 98, 111, 117, 121, 127, 153, 164, 171, 182
Dominions, 98, 115, 167
Dragon, 27, 152
Dragon's blood., 91
Dragonfly, 179
Dread Lords, 192
East, 65, 191, 206
East Wind, 115, 122
Egregoroi, 187
Elizabeth, 64, 172
El-Shaddai, 208, 210
Emerald, 29, 35, 139, 162, 179
Enoch, 13, 15, 44, 79, 98, 99, 115, 116, 134, 172, 185, 186, 187, 188, 193, 195, 196, 197, 198, 199, 200, 201, 202, 204, 205, 207, 208, 210, 211
Enochian, 220
Ephod, 35
Episcopal Church, 172

Equinox, 190
Ethereal, 39, 55, 73, 110, 163, 189
Ethiopian, 13, 187, 189
Evocation, 15
Exodus, 5
Ezekiel, 5, 29
Fairy, 5
Fallen angels, 6, 30, 31, 99, 188, 189, 191
Feathers, 90, 198, 205
Festival of Lights, 185
Fifth Heaven, 87
Fire, 11, 24, 36, 47, 51, 52, 70, 75, 80, 93, 98, 122, 191, 198, 206
Firmament, 37
First Heaven, 70, 72, 106, 141
Fisherman, 118
Flame of God, 169
Flat earth, 19
Fomalhaut, 190
Foundation, 11, 21, 36, 192, 207
Four quarters, 191, 192
Frankincense, 33, 49, 68, 85, 104, 120, 157, 176
Friday, 32, 134, 136, 137, 215, 216
Fumigation, 56, 75, 92, 111, 127, 147, 163
Gabri'el, 14, 15, 39, 44, 46, 58, 63, 64, 65, 66, 67, 68, 69, 70, 71, 72, 73, 74, 75, 76, 77, 78, 81, 86, 98, 99, 100, 105, 115, 133, 134, 151, 165,

167, 171, 174, 177, 190, 206, 207, 208, 215, 217
Gadre-el, 80
Gala-as, 160
Ga-le-thog, 77
Gardnerian, 192
Garnet, 34
Gatekeeper, 11
Gehenna, 189
Gemini, 102
Genesis, 5, 99, 185, 186, 188, 189
Gethog, 107
Ghost, 10, 77
Ginzberg, Louis, 80
Gnosticism, 81, 152
God, 5, 9, 11, 12, 13, 16, 27, 29, 30, 34, 43, 44, 56, 59, 61, 63, 79, 80, 81, 85, 87, 92, 93, 95, 97, 98, 99, 100, 106, 115, 128, 130, 133, 153, 169, 171, 178, 186, 187, 188, 189
Golden Legend, 134
Golden Wedding, 46
Grand Architect of the universe, 18
Grand Seal of Earth, 3
Graphi'el, 91
Greek, 12, 44, 97, 187, 190, 214
Green paper, 102
Grigori, 15, 171, 187, 188, 191
Grimoire, 6, 12, 222, 223
Guardian angel, 10, 80, 155

Guardian of the Tree of Life, 97
Hagi'el, 145
Halachic Midrashim, 115
Hall, Judy, 24
Hanukkah, 185
Hasmallim, 115
Heaven and hell, 11, 31
Hebrew, 11, 43, 44, 59, 63, 80, 97, 99, 100, 115, 133, 169, 185, 186, 190, 214, 220
Heinrich Cornelius Agrippa, 214
Help, 175
Hemah, 80
Heptagonal, 93
Heptameron, 6
Hermes, 44
Hidden mysteries, 5
Himalayan masters, 11
Hinduism, 11
Hisma'el, 126
Hizki'el, 151
Hod, 206
Holy Spirit, 17
Holy Table, 220
Honesty plant, 123
Ibis, 102
Incense, 14, 23, 33, 49, 56, 68, 75, 85, 91, 104, 111, 120, 127, 157
Indian yogis, 11
Inhalation, 33, 49, 68, 85, 104, 120, 157, 176
Inner voices, 34, 50, 69, 86, 105, 158

Intelligence, 17, 30, 55, 58, 91, 101, 110, 145
Invocation, 14, 15, 18, 21, 35, 50, 69, 87, 105, 117, 121, 140, 158, 174, 177
Irim, 15
Isaac, 43, 80, 116
Isaiah, 28, 133, 191
Ishtar, 134
Islam, 11, 100
Israfel, 100
Italy, 191
Jasmine, 74, 180
Jasper, 29
Jesuits, 220
Jews, 11, 65, 98, 116, 223
Jibril, 65
Joan of Arc, 64
Job, Book of, 6
John the Baptist, 64, 172
Jophi'el, 126
Joy of God, 133
Jubilees, 44, 186, 187, 189
Jude, 189
Judgment, 65
Jupiter, 10, 118, 121, 123, 124, 125, 126, 127, 166, 216
Kamea, 57, 74, 92, 110, 126, 146, 164
Kedemel, 145
Kelley, Edward, 13
Key of Solomon the King, 6
Kiev, 45
King James, 28
Kingdom, 64, 151, 159, 207, 209

Kircher, Athanasius, 220
Kokabi-el, 200
Koran, 65
Labbi'el, 98
Lamen, 60, 210
Latin, 27
Laurel trees, 52
Lavender, 108, 118
Lead pencil, 155
Legend of The Jews, 80
Leitch, Aaron, 3
Leland, Charles, 191
Leonardo da Vinci, 172
Letters, 47
Letters of petition, 31, 47, 66, 83, 102, 118, 137
Libra, 31, 32, 136, 137
Lightning flash, 78, 94, 173
Lil'ith, 81
Lilac, 123
Lilly, 108
Lilly of the Valley, 108
Lobelia, 126
Longfellow, 134
Lords of the Watchtowers, 191
Love, 5, 14, 16, 23, 25, 31, 34, 37, 50, 66, 69, 73, 86, 105, 117, 121, 153, 174
Love birds, 142
Luc'ifer, 16, 27, 28, 29, 30, 31, 32, 34, 35, 36, 37, 38, 39, 40, 41, 50, 52, 55, 56, 57, 58, 59, 60, 62, 69, 70, 73, 75, 77, 78, 79, 86, 88, 91, 92,

93, 94, 95, 105, 110, 112, 116, 121, 123, 124, 127, 128, 129, 130, 134, 136, 140, 141, 147, 149, 158, 160, 163, 165, 167, 177, 179, 181, 182, 211, 215

Luna, 166

Lunar month, 32, 137

Lychees, 74

Ma'adim, 89

Machen, 53

Machon, 87, 89

Magic circle, 192

Magic Seal of Dr John Dee, 220

Magical help, 32, 67, 84, 103, 137, 156

Magical Intentions, 45, 82, 117, 136, 154

Magical personality, 25

Magus, 12, 14

Magus or Celestia Intelligencer, 152

Mal'akh, 11

Mal-kuth, 207

Marjoram, 108

Mark of healing, 109

Mars, 10, 17, 82, 83, 88, 89, 90, 92, 166, 215, 222

Mary, 64, 172, 173

Matthew, 153, 222

Mazlot, 180

Mecca, 65

Meditation, 25, 59, 76, 93, 111, 128, 154, 165

Mercury, 10, 43, 97, 102, 107, 108, 110, 111, 166, 215

Merkabah, 170

Messenger, 11, 69, 106

Messiah, 172

Metatron, 80, 82, 134, 186

Methuselah, 185

Midrash Rabbah, 170

Midrashic, 44

Mikh'ael, 14, 15, 16, 39, 43, 44, 45, 46, 47, 48, 49, 51, 54, 55, 56, 58, 59, 60, 62, 63, 81, 86, 98, 99, 100, 105, 116, 128, 134, 166, 167, 171, 174, 177, 190, 215, 217

Mikh'aelmas Day, 45

Milton, John, 100

Miracles, 175

Mirrors, 101, 107

Mocoton, 152

Mohammed, 65

Molinet, Jean, 44

Monday, 67, 215

Money, 118

Monkey Puzzle, 88

Monkeys, 107

Moon, 10, 65, 67, 69, 70, 72, 73, 74, 108, 125, 133, 160, 202

Morning star, 28

Moses, 43, 44, 64, 80, 186, 223

Moslems, 65

Mount Hermon, 196, 197, 198, 199

Mount of Curses, 197

Mount Sinai, 44
Musk, 143, 180, 216
Myrrh, 56
Mystics, 5, 6
Nag Hammadi library, 81
Nakhi'el, 55
Narcissus, 107, 123
Nehemiah, 185
Neo-Pagan, 192
Nephilim, 15, 99, 171, 187, 188, 189
New Age, 5
New Testament, 28
Noah, 99, 171, 185, 189
North, 29, 160
North and East, 106
Northern, 141, 159, 160, 162, 207
Northern Portal, 207
Northern Rivers, 141
Numbers, 61, 74, 77, 92, 127, 148, 149, 182, 185
Oak, 123, 161
Oil, 33, 49, 68, 85, 104, 120, 139, 157, 176, 193
Old Ones, 192
Old Testament, 5, 7
Olive, 43
Olympic spirit, 126
Onyx, 29
Ophelia, 179
Oppression, 154
Order of St Mikh'ael, 45
Orphid, 63
Outer Spaces, 192
Owl, 74

Paper, 155
Paradise, 20
Paradise Lost, 100, 172
Paratroopers, 45
Parrot, 161
Passage du Fleuve, 214
Passing the Rivers Script, 32
Path, 46, 53, 117
Pathworking, 25, 31, 47, 66, 83, 102, 118
patriarch, 116
Patriarchs, 185
Pauline Arts, 6
Peace, 5, 6, 31, 40, 43, 55, 62, 78, 95, 98, 113, 117, 131, 182, 187
PELE, 59
Pentagram, 82, 165, 166, 167, 174
Perfume, 24
Persia, 64
Peter, 28
Phaleg, 91
Physical Realm, 40
Piazza Esedra, 172
Picture Museum of Sorcery, Magic and Alchemy, 152
Pillar of fire, 11
Pink paper, 32, 137
Pipes, 29
Pisces, 118
Planet, 6, 10, 17, 18, 27, 54, 72, 74, 82, 83, 89, 101, 108, 118, 122, 124, 136, 143, 154, 160, 180, 181, 191, 202

Poison, 79
Pomegranate, 126
Pope, 172, 223
Pope St Zachary, 171
Poppy, 123, 163
Positive aspects, 31
Prayer, 14, 33, 49, 68, 85, 104, 117, 120, 133, 157, 176, 193
Prayers, 14
Prince, 44, 79, 191
Principalities, 134
Prison, 83
Prophesy, 101
Prostitution, 81
Proverbs, 185
Psalm, 185
Psychopomp, 44
Pumpkin, 126
Purple ink, 47, 118
Quartz, 16, 34, 50, 69, 86, 105, 121, 158, 177, 211, 215
Queen bee, 123
Queen Elizabeth 1st, 12
Rabbi Abba, 98
Rabbi Eliezer, 80
Rabbi Ishmael ben Elisha, 187
Rainbow, 181
Rami-el, 200
Rapha'el, 15, 44, 63, 64, 81, 97, 98, 99, 100, 101, 102, 103, 104, 105, 106, 107, 108, 109, 110, 111, 112, 113, 114, 134, 166, 167, 171, 174, 177, 190, 206, 208, 215, 217, 218
Ra-quia, 108
Rashi, 186
Realm, 51, 56, 59, 62, 69, 70, 75, 78, 87, 92, 95, 105, 106, 111, 113, 122, 127, 130, 159, 163, 178, 182
Realm of Chaos, 38
Red ink, 32, 84, 137
Regulus, 190
Religion, 11
Rembrandt, 100, 116
Rephaim, 189
Resurrection, 11
Revelation, 5
Righteousness of God', 115
Ring, 16, 34, 50, 59, 60, 61, 69, 75, 86, 93, 94, 100, 105, 112, 123, 125, 128, 130, 148, 158, 164, 177, 206, 210
Robe, 21
Rome, 80
Rose, 47
Ruling Angels, 175
Sabaoth, 52
Safra Rabba, 186
Sagittarius, 118
Salamander, 51
Sama'el, 15, 79, 80, 81, 82, 83, 84, 85, 86, 87, 88, 89, 90, 91, 92, 93, 95, 96, 99, 105, 134, 166, 177, 215, 217, 218
Sandalwood, 74, 107, 143, 146, 215, 216

Santa Maria del Angeli, 172
Sapphire, 29, 35, 215
Sardius, 29
Sarim, 152
Sata-el, 200
Satan, 27, 29, 79, 98, 191, 222
Satan Kanom', 79
Saturday, 155, 174, 216
Saturn, 10, 17, 152, 154, 155, 158, 160, 161, 162, 163, 164, 166, 216
Scented oil, 24
Sceptre, 125, 126, 130
Science, 101
Scorpio, 83
Scorpion, 83
Scotland, 45
Scribe, 12, 187
Scrying, 220
Sea, 37, 66, 118
Seagull, 74
Seal, 41, 62, 78, 90, 94, 95, 114, 125, 130, 131, 149, 150, 168, 183, 219
Seal of Truth, 3, 19, 93, 112, 148, 165, 220
Seals, 7
Second Heaven, 108, 141
Secret Grimoire of Turiel, 13
Secret name, 32
Secrets, 11
Secrets of Heaven', 65
Sefer Hekalot, 187
Sefer Noah, 99
Sefer Razi'el, 99

Semitic gods, 10
Sephirah of Netzach, 136
Seraphim, 79, 106
Serenity, 85
Serpent, 58, 80, 98, 110
Servants of the Light Mystery School, 22
Set, 27, 189
Seth, 185
Seven divine beings, 11
Seventh Heaven, 63
Shakespeare, William, 134
Shamain, 72
Sheep, 45, 92, 203
Shehaqim, 141, 143
Shellfish, 74
Shem-esh, 54
Shemyaza, 187, 188, 199, 200, 205
Shield, 54, 56, 95, 201
Shield of David, 60
Shlomo Yitzhaki, 187
Sigillvm Dei Æmæth: Emeth, 219
Sigils, 7
Sigilum dei Aemeth, 3
Silver Birch, 107
Sixth Heaven, 122
Sodom and Gomorrah, 5, 64
Solar, 46, 86, 107, 140, 190
Solar Systems, 160
Solomon, 13, 60, 75, 93, 100, 112, 128, 147, 164, 223
Solstice, 190, 191

Sons of Darkness, 43
Sons of Light, 43
Sons of the Sons, 20
Sorath, 55
Sorcery, 152
South, 47, 63, 70, 122, 162, 171, 172, 178
South America, 172
Southern Portal, 206
Spanish, 172
Speed of God, 151
Spells, 213
Spirit, 13, 14, 16, 34, 50, 58, 69, 75, 81, 86, 98, 105, 121, 172, 177, 189, 191
Spirit of Spirits of the Moon, 73
spiritual journey, 116
Spiritualist's, 11
splendour, 206
Spruce, 123
St George, 44
St Michael's Bannock, 45
St Mikh'ael, 44
St. Thomas Aquinas, 9
Star, 27, 28, 37, 39, 40, 89, 100, 109, 134, 148, 190, 191, 202, 210
Star-forms, 148
Stellar, 40, 190
Sterility, 66
Strength, 33, 45, 49, 63, 68, 82, 83, 85, 104, 120, 152, 157, 176, 206
Sulphur, 86, 89, 140
Sulphuric acid, 36
Sumerian, 10

Summa Theologiae1a, 192
Summon, 15
Sun, 10, 46, 52, 97
Sunday, 43, 46, 47, 97, 215
Sunflowers, 52
Supreme, 117
Supreme Creator, 11
Supreme Universal Lord, 11
Surgery, 82
Suri'el, 44
Swan, 118
Sword, 47, 54, 55, 56, 75, 82, 83, 90, 116, 167
Symbols, 31, 32, 47, 61, 66, 70, 83, 94, 102, 107, 113, 118, 142, 155
Tabard, 60, 75, 93, 112, 128, 147, 165
Table, 60, 74, 111, 126, 163, 220
Table of the Sun, 57
Talbot, Sir Edward, 13
Talisman, 14, 54, 56, 72, 109, 221
Talmud, 80
Talmudic, 43, 79
Tam-i-el, 201
Taph-thart-har-ath, 110
Targum Yerushalmi, 186
Tartarus, 171
Taurus, 31, 136
Teachers, 65
Tempest, 134
Terry Hill, 3
Testament of Solomon, 100

Tetragrammaton, 52
Tha-aoth, 88
Tharsis and Elysium, 88
The Ascension of Moses, 80
The Holy Kabbalah, 81
The Queen's Conjuror, 14
Theban Script, 47
Thebe, 122
Theosophists, 11
Third Heaven, 178
Thoth, 102
Throne, 28, 30, 39, 54, 55, 56, 98, 170
Throne Angel, 174
Throne of God, 17
Thursday, 117, 119, 216
Tigris and Euphrates Rivers, 10
Timbrels, 29
Tiphareth, 206
Tiri'el, 110
tobacco leaf, 91
Tobias, 99
Tobit, 64, 99
Topaz, 29, 35, 215
Tortoise, 161
Travel, 65, 66, 78, 101
Truth, 9, 25, 36, 37, 40, 43, 98
Tuesday, 84, 215
Turiel, 222
Turquoise, 29
Ultra-violet, 121
Underworld, 97
Ura-kiba, 200, 202, 205

Uranus, 17, 173, 178, 179, 181, 182, 216
Uri'el, 13, 15, 44, 46, 78, 81, 94, 98, 134, 154, 167, 169, 170, 171, 172, 173, 174, 175, 176, 177, 178, 180, 181, 182, 183, 190, 206, 207, 208, 216, 217
Valerian, 126
Vaporizer, 24
Venom, 79
Venom of God, 79, 85
Venus, 10, 28, 31, 36, 133, 134, 135, 136, 140, 141, 142, 143, 145, 146, 149, 166, 215, 216
Verbena, 108, 146, 215, 216
Ver-eth-ragna, 197
Violet, 143
virgin, 101
Virgin, 65, 102
Virgo, 101, 102
Visualization, 7
vitality, 176
Vitality, 33, 49, 68, 85, 104, 120, 157
Voice of Angels, 32
Volcanic, 88, 93, 171
Vowel sounds, 208
Waite, Arthur Edward, 81
Walpole, Horace, 221
Wand, 74, 147, 173, 181, 182, 210
War in Heaven', 27
Warrior, 45, 47, 98, 116
Warts, 21, 66

Watcher of the North, 190
Watcher of the South, 190
Watcher of the West, 190
Watchers, 171, 187, 188, 195
Watchtowers, 191, 192
Wax, 60, 61, 76, 93, 94, 112, 113, 129, 130, 148, 149, 165, 198, 220
Wedding, 95
Wednesday, 101, 102, 215
West, 66
Western and Southern Rivers, 87
Western Portal, 207
Whale, 118
White paper, 32, 67, 84, 118, 137
White peacock, 74
Wiccan, 191, 192
Willow, 74
Winged beings, 9, 12, 19
Winter, 66, 81
Wisdom, 29, 37, 38, 101, 110, 154, 158
Wisdom of Sirach, 187
Wise, Caroline, 3
Witchcraft, 192
Witches, 191, 213

Women, 65, 66, 200
Wrath, 5, 6, 197, 199
Writing, 12, 19, 28, 31, 32, 47, 66, 67, 83, 84, 99, 101, 102, 118, 119, 155, 186, 213
Yahweh, 44
Yalkut, 80
Yellow paper, 47
Yesod, 207
Yetzirah, 136
Yew, 161
Yomi-el, 201
Zachari'el, 81
Zadki'el, 15, 115, 116, 117, 118, 119, 120, 121, 122, 123, 124, 125, 126, 127, 128, 129, 130, 131, 166, 177, 216, 217
Zaqi-el, 201
Zazel, 163
Zebul, 122, 124
Zechariah, 64
Zeitgeist, 81
Zeus, 118
Zodiac, 31, 83, 155, 174
Zohar, 98, 133, 170
Zoroastrians, 10, 11

www.ingramcontent.com/pod-product-compliance
Ingram Content Group UK Ltd.
Pitfield, Milton Keynes, MK11 3LW, UK
UKHW052309050126
466610UK00012B/52